# THE BREAKFAST CLUB FOR 40-SOMETHINGS

# THE BREAKFAST CLUB FOR 40-SOMETHINGS

A Novel Approach to
Unlearning Money and
Reinventing Your Life

VANESSA STOYKOV

WILEY

First published in 2018 by John Wiley & Sons Australia, Ltd
42 McDougall St, Milton Qld 4064
Office also in Melbourne

Typeset in 12/14pt Adobe Garamond Pro

© John Wiley & Sons Australia, Ltd 2018

The moral rights of the author have been asserted

A catalogue record for this book is available from the National Library of Australia

Cover design by Paul McCarthy

Cover image Getty Images/MARIUSFM77

In creating this book, the author has been inspired by the movie *The Breakfast Club* directed by John Hughes and produced by Ned Tanen (1985), A&M Films & Channel Productions (US). However, the author and publisher wish to note that this book is not endorsed by, affiliated with or associated with this movie, its producers, copyright owners or other related parties in any way.

Printed in the United States

V00180_050418

**Disclaimer**

*For my father, Tom, who always knew I could.*
*For my mother, Sue, who insisted I should.*
*For my husband, Paul, who makes all things good.*
*And for my sons, Sebastian, Connor and Harrison —*
*quite simply, my life.*

# Contents

# Prologue

All of our thoughts and actions towards money are influenced by our past; by our parents, our upbringing, our community and peers; even by magazines, media and the world around us. But what if some of the things you 'know' about money are the very things holding you back?

After 24 years as a journalist and educator in the financial services industry, and by reflecting on my own *unlearning* experiences, I have realised that five big lessons around money hold people back from having financial freedom — in whatever form that means for them. These lessons need to be *unlearned* before people can actually *learn* how to better use what money they *do* have to reach their goals.

# What's holding you back?

My top five lessons people need to unlearn about money all revolve around five powerful pillars, as shown in the following figure.

Let's explore each of these pillars in detail.

## *Desire*

This is a big one in Western society. This pillar is all about the lure of having things that are *wants* rather than needs. We all do it—from clothes, cars, gadgets and eating out to bags and shoes—I'm talking here about whatever your *thing* is that you love to spend on.

And when I say this needs to be unlearned, I am not talking about eliminating desire entirely (where is the fun in that?) but rather learning to make decisions around the things that are investments in your happiness, and those that trap you with debt and, therefore, stress and unhappiness.

## *Focus*

Sometimes it's hard to paint the picture in your mind of what it is you truly want. And usually you have to reach a certain age (mostly in your 40s) before you can start to think about this — to have enough life experience to truly understand what brings you happiness and what really matters. When you have clarity around how you want to live long term, you can then start to make a plan toward it.

Without that long-term clarity, however, most of us go from thing to thing, job to job and holiday to holiday, looking for happiness and finding nothing more than moments. Unlearning vague wants and unarticulated desires and getting clarity are critical to achieving your financial prosperity.

## *Time*

The impact that time has on our thinking around money should not be underestimated. When we are young, we think retirement is far away; as we get to middle age, we feel we have so many demands on our money that time keeps slipping away.

We make decisions based on truly not understanding the impact of time—like looking for fast money via gambling, or ignoring our super because we can't get it for years anyway. The way most of us look at time has a huge impact on our financial wellbeing.

## *Belief*

What we intrinsically believe about money usually turns out to be true. Do you believe that you never have enough? That too much is not a good thing? That it slips through your fingers?

Your belief or mindset around money is definitely learned from childhood. How to change these beliefs is part psychology and part self-examination. Many of us have deep-rooted beliefs that hold us back from our true potential.

## *Action*

Many of us have learned our financial actions from our parents—for example, buy a house, put money in the bank. But are these actions the best ones for you to gain financial freedom?

By understanding your options, and the need to have different strategies around your money for long- and short-term goals in your life, you can truly develop an action plan that sees you achieve exactly what you want.

*Please note, this book is a tribute to the movie,* The Breakfast Club, *but it isn't in any way associated with, or endorsed by, the producers or copyright owners of the movie, or any other related parties.*

# Novel beginnings

Now comes the fun part. I get to tell you a story. Meet 'The Breakfast Club for 40-Somethings'. Here are characters we can all relate to, because we either are a bit like them, or know people who are. (And if you know me, rest assured that none of these characters is modelled on you! Rather, they are a combination of years of interviewing and people watching, and researching the psychological effects that money has on people's behaviour.) These characters are also a lot like me in many ways—this has been a journey of self-assessment!

When you recognise yourself in a character, take special note. Perhaps their unlearn lessons are exactly the same as the ones you need to unlearn yourself. A lot of them have been mine.

Most of all, take note of the decisions that the characters make—either consciously or unconsciously—and think about how they grew up, what place they hold in society now, and how they view themselves. All these aspects will have greatly affected their decisions, regardless of whether these decisions were right or wrong.

Every one of us is living our own story—and how we end it is up to us. My hope is that by reading this book you may choose to plan your ending a little differently, and not leave it to chance.

Join these six friends as they figure it all out. It's *The Breakfast Club for 40-Somethings.*

# Meet the characters

The story revolves around six main characters (plus one handy financial planner). Let's get to know the six a bit better before launching in.

## *Karen and Russ Douglas*

These guys are high-school sweethearts who are still together. While from the outside they look like they have the perfect life, things are not always as they seem, and Karen and Russ face challenges that are familiar to so many of us — juggling parenting, ageing parents, money pressures and work hassles.

Here are their vital stats:

- married for 17 years
- three kids (two at private school)
- Karen runs the home while Russ works in accounting for $220 000 a year
- mortgage of $700 000, with a house value of $2.5 million
- credit card debt of $28 000
- Karen has $22 000 in super and Russ has more than $180 000
- no real savings, only a few thousand dollars.

## *Josephine*

This is a woman who looks like she has it all. Driven and ambitious, Josephine has built a business around her unique skill set in communicating. But Josephine hides a secret about the reality of her life. One that threatens to ruin everything she has built.

Her vital stats are:

- business turns over more than $10 million
- pulls $500 000 salary, plus bonus of $500 000
- no kids and not married
- five properties — heavily leveraged with debt
- business is 'key woman dependent' and 'key client dependent'
- high overheads and a need for strong cash flow.

## Jasper

Jasper is the perennial good time guy. He's an athlete who peaked in potential in high school. He never holds down a job for too long and drinks more than he should — but he is a likeable guy with a kind heart. And he's starting to wonder what will become of him ...

Here are Jasper's vital stats:

- single, never married
- lives with his mum
- low income earner, with plenty of down times, no fixed salary
- $50 000 in super, and no savings
- finds it hard to manage money.

## Jayne

Jayne's smart, bubbly and an expert in juggling — being a working mum with two kids. Since her divorce from her unreliable and volatile ex-husband, she relies on her parents a lot to help out. She works in the law, but her real ambition lies elsewhere ...

Jayne's vital stats are:

- single mother of two girls
- $90 000 salary plus super
- $80 000 in super
- owns no property, renting her home
- unreliable ex and seeking a new partner.

## Brad

Brad is a billionaire tech genius. He remains bitter towards his parents, however — particularly his mother, who pushed him to be an overachiever as a child. Their relationship is strained.

Brad's no longer motivated by money, but doesn't want to lose in business. For him, money is a scorecard.

Here are Brad's vital stats:

- billionaire CEO of global company
- not married, no kids
- known as a tough and distant leader.

So now you know who everyone is, let's get started on their stories.

# Chapter 1

# Karen

*Dammit,* thought Karen as she stared at the stain on her son's shirt, *I only washed that yesterday.* This was a common thought in the Douglas household—three kids, in varying ages from year 4 to year 10, tended to generate a lot of stains.

*I bet Josie isn't thinking about laundry,* Karen thought with a touch of envy. *She'll be thinking about what she's going to wear for the school reunion.* She smiled, imagining the lengths her friend of more than 30 years would go to in order to make a splash at their 25-year reunion.

These last thoughts quickly brought her back to her own predicament. The 13 kilograms she'd gained since having three kids meant that, at 43, she was looking for jeans with high waists and tummy control. The muffin top spilling out from the low-rise jeans that everyone wore now was just too hard to disguise.

She had always been the pretty one at school and, while she was still considered attractive, she was no teenager either—and she just didn't have the time or the inclination to work on herself the way Josie did. Of course, the fact Josie had no kids and wasn't married made it all a bit easier for her. With three kids and a house to run, Karen just didn't get the chance for much self-maintenance.

At times it was tough having a best friend who was so glamorous and, as they got older, Karen felt that even more. When they did manage to go out to dinner or catch a movie together, men still stared at Josie—and usually none of those men gave her a second look.

'It doesn't matter anyway,' she told herself and shrugged, in her good-natured way. 'Russ still looks at me like I am the goods, and that's all that ever really mattered to me.'

She had been married to Russ for seventeen years now—married in their twenties, after getting together in high school. They'd been the couple in year 12 that everyone had predicted would get married and have kids. She'd always been proud that they'd lived up to that.

She was also proud they'd made something of themselves. They bought a house early, at age 33. And by diligently renovating bit by bit for the past 10 years, they'd made some amazing gains. While they still had what Karen thought was a big mortgage—$700 000—she knew that the house must be worth well over $2 million now. The neighbours had just sold for $2.3 million anyway and, in her opinion, their yard was nowhere near as good as her own—and she had four bedrooms, not three.

But they still had a long way to go before they owned it. Russ worked back late most nights at an accounting firm in the city. 'Getting ahead,' he told Karen, as he steadily climbed pay grades. He was now on more than $220 000.

*I'm proud of him*, Karen thought. For a boy whose parents wanted him to learn a trade and get a job after year 10, Russ had had the self-discipline to be more ambitious. He studied through to year 12, did very well in the HSC and went on to university to study accounting and actuarial studies. And the whole time Russ had to work part-time to support himself because his parents couldn't. At uni, Russ would pour beers in a club in the city and average about four hours sleep a night.

He did it tough but he got through it, and his current salary was a reflection of that hard work.

Karen's parents, on the other hand, were pleased that she had become a full-time mum — that's all they ever expected of her, and they loved that she was such a great mother. They lived in a semi on the central coast and their grandchildren were their pride and joy. Karen made sure to take the kids to visit once a month, for a weekend away. While staying with her parents was not exactly a holiday, when Russ was working it was something to do with the kids that didn't cost a bomb.

While Karen finished off the laundry, Russ walked in the front door. 'Hello, wife, you're looking hot today,' he said, as he grabbed Karen cheekily on the backside.

'Get out of it.' She playfully swatted his hand away. She loved that Russ still fancied her after all these years, and she knew in her heart that he would never cheat on her. It just wasn't in him.

'I've got a plan, Karen, and you are going to love it,' he said excitedly as he threw his briefcase down on the lounge chair. Karen felt a tinge of annoyance — there was a hall table for bags — but decided to let it go. After all, her husband was in a spectacular mood, and seeing this made her happy.

She had started to worry about him for the past few months. He'd seemed more stressed, more stretched than she had ever seen him. She knew his stress was to do with work, but he'd also lost some of that boyish spark that had made her fall in love with him. While usually so optimistic, he was now seeing things with a tinge of grey. Often he seemed distracted and distant for much of the week.

She knew his state of mind was not great, but she had no idea how to change it for him. She already carried pretty much all the load of the kids and running a household. She was the taxi driver, shopper, housekeeper and cleaner. In fact, as she grappled with trying to make everything as perfect as she should, she often felt exhausted. While she sometimes resented everything she had taken on, she continued to push herself. After all, her family deserved it.

Their kids were a reflection of the love and attention they had been given. They were, in fact, her pride and joy, not just their grandparents'.

Nate, her sixteen-year-old eldest son, was a constant source of parental pride. He was serious, with a strong sense of right and wrong. As well as being unwaveringly fair, he was also kind and responsible—always helping when he knew it was needed, and mostly doing the right thing. He did well at school, and was on track to getting a science degree, if he kept his grades up, which seemed fairly likely. She was really proud of him.

And Bella, with her Bohemian style, and graceful ways, was a constant surprise. She was amazed at the way her fourteen-year-old daughter had turned out so far. *I don't know where she comes from*, Karen thought with wonder. Bella was not just beautiful but also naturally stylish, and incredibly kind. All of which meant people were drawn to her, and Karen worried that she would be taken advantage of as she got older—she was sure to be a target for boys and men with her looks and trusting personality.

And then there was Taz, with his cheeky blue eyes and impish grin. That kid was impossible not to love. He was all mischief and pranks and, at ten years old, was a popular kid at his primary school. His love of fun and his good-natured ways meant he was always being asked to play dates and parties. His social life kept Karen very busy.

Karen felt extremely lucky to have three amazing children. No matter how tired she became, or how desperately she sometimes wanted to be alone, if her kids needed her, she was present. There. They were the most important people in her life. Giving them opportunities and attention was not only her job; it was also her reason for being…which was a little scary. Because she knew that reason for being would not last forever. Her kids were growing up fast. Even the fact that Nate was thinking about university courses blew her mind. Imagine! Her son would soon be moving out and having his own life. She knew it was coming and, in a way, had realised that the teenage years provided an opportunity to prepare for the day they moved out.

Nate had become more distant over the past couple of years—involved heavily with texting his friends when home, and wanting to spend a lot of time in his room with the door closed. She missed her little boy, the one who used to include her as he embraced life and saw her and Russ, and his siblings, as his whole world.

She let herself remember for a minute all the gorgeous moments when her first born swelled her heart with love. *What a gift to be a mother*, she thought with a smile.

But back to her husband—what was he so excited about?

# Chapter 2

# Russ

Russ felt Karen's attention turn back to him. *I bet she was thinking about the kids again*, he thought, with a touch of annoyance. It was hard to get much 'head time' with his wife once the three kids had come along. She was an incredible mother, and he was constantly grateful for that, but she was also very focused on them as her priority.

Russ knew that she loved him — she told him often enough and he believed her. But her passion and focus was definitely the kids and, if he cared to admit it, this made him feel lonely sometimes.

He knew he wasn't great at keeping up with his friends. He thought of them, of course, but never actually got around to sending a text, or catching up for a beer that often. He was pretty useless like that. He always vowed that he would make more of an effort and, when he did get to see friends, he enjoyed it greatly.

He especially loved seeing his oldest friend from high school, Jasper. The eternal good time guy, who always seemed to be catching a big one, or going on this adventure or another. *Lucky bugger*, Russ thought ruefully, as he prepared to tell his wife about his new plan and the new challenge that would make his world much more fulfilling.

For the most part, he liked what he did. But, more and more, the company culture was tougher to take. If he was honest, Russ had been struggling with it for months. His days were feeling longer and longer, and having to smile and accept what increasingly seemed a culture of self-interest and politics was not his style at all.

He knew it was time to leave there and look at somewhere new. At 43, he was still young enough to make a successful career change and establish himself somewhere else. He wasn't beyond doing more study again, either. Maybe he could branch out of accounting and into funds management. The investing industry made him feel a surge of excitement. A new challenge. New people—and new energy. It would also mean more money. He couldn't keep his thoughts from his wife any longer.

'I'm going to quit my job,' Russ blurted out gleefully. Goodbye to that bad vibe office, and the feeling of dread that filled him more and more often at the thought of getting out of bed for work when the 6 am alarm went off.

He had expected Karen to be surprised at this announcement, but what he was seeing before him was a different reaction.

'Why? What's happened?' she cried, eyes widening.

'Well, nothing,' said Russ, becoming instantly aware that her mood wasn't following his exhilarated one.

'Thank God,' she exhaled, looking relieved.

'Does something need to happen for me to be allowed to quit a job I hate, one I've done for thirteen years, and find something that actually makes me happy?' he snapped, his voice harsher than he'd intended.

Karen instantly recoiled and looked mortified that she'd made him unhappy. That too annoyed him. Sometimes he wished she was just up for a good old-fashioned fight, and that she'd say what she really thought, rather than backing down and bottling it up. He suspected that was one of the reasons she was always hitting the chocolates and treats — to stop things being said that she thought shouldn't.

Russ sighed, knowing that Karen was worried about money. And he also knew that she had to. She was not a woman who spent money on herself very often, he certainly acknowledged that. In fact, when he splurged and bought her a piece of jewellery, or something worth more than a few hundred dollars, he could tell it worried her. She knew the financial position they were in, and most likely felt that the money was better spent elsewhere rather than on her.

Karen not being able to enjoy a few splurges made him feel bad. She deserved gifts, and much more. She had been his rock and his support since high school, and he knew deep down the life they had, and the way their kids had turned out, were all because of Karen.

He didn't want her to have to worry about money. He should be earning more than enough to keep his family happy. And he would have that potential if he found the next job — he was sure he could earn at least another $50k or even $100k with a job move.

All this brought him back to his plan. He would quit ASAP.

Karen had been watching his face. 'I want you to be happy, and I think it's a great idea for you to have another challenge. I'm just thinking about the money, babe,' she quickly assured him.

In his heart, he knew what she was suggesting without him even having to ask. And she was right. He couldn't give notice without finding another job. As much as he would love to walk off into the sunset and pursue his next great challenge, he also knew he was responsible for more people than just himself. Four other people lived off the income he made, and he never wanted his family to go without. It was just that sometimes that responsibility felt like a massive rock on his back.

He had grown up with parents who had pounded into him that taking care of your family financially was a man's responsibility. His dad was a mechanic—always working long hours, and drinking even harder when he got home. His mum, it seemed, was everything else. She was the reason Russ even got the chance to make it through year 12—she wanted more for her son than she'd ever had herself. She fought endlessly with his father over it.

He never wanted to let her down—and his drive, hard work and resulting salary success was one of his ways of thanking his long-suffering mum for believing in him. He often put $100 in her bank account as a surprise, which he knew was more than appreciated. His dad had died a few years back, and Mum did it tough in a housing commission flat, living on the pension. He wished he could do more.

But back to being the responsible one with his own family, and reassuring his anxious wife. 'Of course I'll wait till I have found the next gig.' He gave Karen a quick kiss on the lips, which instantly defused the situation.

'Thanks babe.' She smiled as she hugged him hard, relieved she was not going to have to face dodging bills.

'What's for dinner?' Russ asked, starving, expecting something delicious judging by the smell coming from the kitchen.

'Beef stroganoff,' Karen replied, turning toward the kitchen to attend to it.

# Chapter 3

# An invitation

Karen didn't want to fight with Russ about him getting a new job. It was just she knew their financial situation better than him. They had two kids in private school, costing more than $17 000 for each child annually, and with Taz going when Nate finished. Add in the mortgage and living costs, and they couldn't afford to miss a single month's pay.

Their credit cards were already racked up, with another $10k going on to pay for their last holiday to Fiji, on top of the $18k she had already spent over the past few years. She kept paying off the minimum payment but, somehow, the card balance never went down.

Karen quickly reassured herself whenever she felt a pinprick of guilt about the debt. She was sick of waiting until they had saved enough money to go on an overseas trip. The kids were exhausted from school, and school holidays sucked when there was nowhere to go. And it had been a fantastic week in Fiji. They'd all relaxed and had the chance to relate as a family again—without their own individual demands on their time. Those kinds of holidays were essential to keep you together as a family, she had always felt.

But it meant they were maxed out. They could always put nice food on the table, and the kids always got their activities and opportunities — Karen always made sure that was the case, no matter what she went without.

She knew Russ wondered where all the money went. He earned a small fortune but the fact was, in Sydney, $220k didn't really go that far. They drove a nice car and had a second run about; life was comfortable, they lived in a great house, their kids were getting a good education. That was where the money went.

If Russ left his job without securing other income, how was she going to come up with their monthly expenses and string things out? She paid all the bills in the house, and knew exactly what their financial position was on any given day as far as money in the bank. She knew Russ had little clue, apart from a quick look at the credit card statement at the end of the month. He took money out of the ATM when he needed to, and left the rest up to Karen.

While she enjoyed the element of control it gave her, at times it felt like a burden or an unfair responsibility. Should we pay this bill, or that one, before pay day? How long could she string out the excursion fees until it hit end of month?

Their finances were always a juggle, but she always got there in the end. She just did not need her juggling system to be derailed by having no money in the door on a regular basis

Karen focused back on what she needed to be doing. It was almost 6, and the older kids would soon be home from their various co-curricular activities. Taz was already in his room playing with Lego, which he adored, while Nate was coming home from coding and Bella from basketball.

Dinner time was family time in the Douglas house — no TV and no phones were allowed. It was the one time of the day when the whole family sat together and talked. Sure, some days the conversation was better than others, but it meant a lot to Karen and Russ to check in as a family.

Karen rushed to get the pasta on as she heard the door slam twice, signalling the arrival of her eldest children. 'Hi you two,' she yelled, as she continued to go about getting dinner ready.

'Hi Ma,' muttered Nate as he rushed into the kitchen to see what was cooking.

'Stop pinching the pasta,' said Karen indignantly as she turned to see Nate spearing at least ten bow ties from the pot.

'Starving Ma,' he said as he backed out of the kitchen to get showered and ready for dinner.

'Hello Mummy,' smiled Bella, as she kissed Karen on the cheek and wafted away, phone in hand.

'Dinner in 15 minutes,' Karen warned, focus already back on making sure the beef was cooked just right and she'd added enough sour cream to make the sauce as creamy as the kids liked it.

Karen took her cooking very seriously—it was the one way she showed her family night after night how much they meant to her. She did it for them, not herself. While they all believed she loved doing the cooking, most of the time she longed to just make herself a bowl of cereal and watch TV at night, rather than cooking and cleaning up after a whole big meal. But the kids and Russ loved a good dinner, and it really was the one time their family could all come together.

Karen would have loved to have gone out to dinner more. She truly loved being with her family eating out—where she could enjoy someone else cooking her a meal and clearing it all away. She felt more fun—rather than the person who was always rushing and always stressing about spilled milk and cold potatoes.

They had already gone out twice this month, however, and with the five of them, it was at least $120 to eat out somewhere like Chinese. They'd already blown almost $300, and she knew she needed to continue to cook at home if she didn't want to rack that credit card up any further.

Russ returned in his track pants and Taz emerged from his room, asking Karen to check out his latest Lego invention—completed without a plan, Taz proudly told her.

He was a clever boy and Karen made the appropriate noises of appreciation for his creation but, if she was completely honest, she never really had the time to look properly at any of her son's inventions. She was just too darn busy making it all happen.

Taz shrugged his shoulders and headed toward the dinner table. He knew he could count on Mum to make him a yum dinner, and he usually got something pretty good for dessert too—and that was awesome.

When they were all settled at the table, each of them had a turn at talking about something that happened during their day.

Nate shared a story about someone who had beaten him in his latest science assessment. He was obviously disappointed with this, but it reminded Karen again of how competitive and self-motivated her eldest son was.

'Competition is good for the soul, my boy,' said Russ, and Nate nodded seriously.

Meanwhile Bella talked about a gorgeous golden retriever she'd patted at the basketball fields, and once again asked could they get a dog.

'Nobody cleans up after the cat we have,' Karen moaned, once again reminding her daughter she wasn't keen to pick up dog poop as well as clean out the litter tray. Not to mention pets were expensive—the damn cat had cost a fortune this year with its vaccinations and special dietary food.

'I'll do it,' wheedled Bella, to which they all laughed. Bella could barely manage to pull the doona up on her bed.

When it came to Russ's turn, he told everyone how he was starting the search for a new career—and would hopefully be earning more money.

'Cool, will we be rich?' cried Taz, thinking deliriously about more Lego for him.

'Not rich, but we could go on more overseas holidays,' enthused Russ, making all three kids look extremely pleased.

'Ah, maybe we should wait and see about that,' said Karen, ever the killjoy, but thinking it would be good if they put a bit more money in super—after all, she'd left work as soon as she had Nate, and had really only had a few years in the workforce as an executive assistant before becoming a full-time mum. All this meant her super balance was just $22000, and she knew she would need a lot more than that to keep her and Russ in the style to which they were accustomed.

How much they would need, exactly, she didn't know. She had a vague idea that they would live off the proceeds of selling the house eventually. But she didn't want to sell it anytime soon. She had worked way too hard on renovating the bathroom and kitchen to be giving up that.

And Russ had super—more than $180000. But she'd heard on the ABC the other day that the average couple needed well over a million dollars to retire on, even if they owned their own house. This filled her with quiet dread and then the urge not to think about it all too deeply—surely it would work itself out.

'Stop being such a downer, Mum,' said Bella, and Russ silently agreed. After all, what on earth was he working so hard for if they couldn't enjoy things like holidays with the kids? He never went on a single holiday with his parents, outside of visiting his grandparents' farm some school holidays. He wanted more for his wife and kids, and was going to damn well provide it.

Karen felt a wave of annoyance roll over her at Bella's comment. The kids had no idea at all how hard she juggled to make ends meet for the life they had. And she knew they weren't saving enough. Some days the weight of responsibility from being the sensible one made her want to scream.

'Let's just focus on Dad's new job search first,' she replied in a brittle voice — as Russ quickly smiled and said, 'Mum's right,' knowing otherwise Karen might start a lecture, a scene he didn't feel like tonight.

Russ deftly turned the conversation to something else, asking Karen to tell them all about the plans for the school reunion. This instantly improved the mood. Karen become engrossed in telling them what she thought Josephine would wear, and how her friend had invited Russ and her to stay in her suite at the Four Seasons in the city after the event.

'Fantastic,' enthused Russ, knowing Josephine spared no expense and it would be top-shelf liquor in the room.

Nate and Bella were responsible enough to look after Taz for the night, so it was decided that Karen and Russ would indeed have a night away in the city for the big 25-year reunion.

'What are you going to wear, Mum?' asked Bella, before offering to look online with Karen for a new outfit.

While Karen didn't want to spend much, she knew her daughter's sense of style was better than her own — and the last thing she wanted was to turn up looking like a frump.

'Excellent,' she enthused, and hurried them all along to finish and clear up the table — she had some online shopping to do.

Russ, on the other hand, quickly retired to the study. He was going to search for some executive recruiters and find out what was out there for a man of his talents.

Nate went to his room to study, leaving Taz to play on his iPad. Karen felt a little guilty about leaving him to stare at a screen, but she wanted to find an outfit, so that would have to do.

As she clicked on the first site, her mobile buzzed. It was Josephine. 'Hey, we're staying with you — it's on!' Karen enthused when she picked up the call.

'Great!' Josephine replied. 'But we have bigger things to talk about. You will never guess who's coming to the reunion.'

'Who?' replied Karen, feeling like a school girl again.

'Brad Malone. The one who got away,' Josie sighed.

Karen gasped. She'd had no idea someone like Brad Malone would be interested in coming back for their 25-year high school reunion. Brad lived in the United States now, and the last article she'd read about him said the tech company he'd created was in negotiations with Elon Musk.

'OMG — that's huge!' Karen cried.

'Totally huge,' Josephine agreed. She'd dated Brad when she was seventeen. He was the first boy she ever slept with and the only one, as far as Karen could tell, who she'd ever really cared about since.

Brad had broken Josie's heart once university ended — after winning an internship in Silicon Valley and leaving the country. At first, he and Josephine had talked and exchanged letters. But soon the letters and calls stopped and any contact dried up — Josephine had not heard from him in over 20 years.

'I need to lose 5 kilos fast,' said Josephine in a sudden panic.

'What?' cried Karen. 'You're already a size 10 — how thin do you want to be?'

'Thinner,' Josephine replied. She had planned to wear her new Prada cocktail dress, with a grey fur and her matching Louis Vuitton heels. But that wouldn't be enough to capture the attention of Brad Malone.

Karen knew she was going to have to endure a hard day of shopping with Josephine, at places she could never afford, for prices she gasped at just thinking about.

'I'll pick you up at 10 tomorrow,' said Josephine, before hanging up.

*Yep, looks like I'm going shopping*, thought Karen — in half excitement and half dread.

This reunion was going to be more interesting than she'd thought. With someone as big as Brad attending, the stakes had gone up. He was one of the few tech billionaires Australia had produced, and word in the gossip pages was he'd just broken up with his latest model girlfriend.

Karen only hoped that Josephine didn't get her hopes up too high. Brad did not seem like the kind of man who came home to find his childhood sweetheart. But why was he coming at all?

# Chapter 4
# Josephine

*This is only round one,* thought Josephine, smiling on the outside as she shook hands with the marketing manager who was rejecting her first approach for a $250 000 event sponsorship.

Josephine knew this one was going to take some work — she seemed to be one of those female middle management marketing people who didn't appreciate other women in business. Josie had seen many over her career — the ones who blocked innovative ideas if they hadn't thought of them, and who distrusted anyone they hadn't installed getting access to their CEO and board.

These women usually went out of their way to make sure opportunities didn't come to Josie. But she'd been playing the game long enough to know how to combat them.

'Always go up,' was usually how Josephine dealt with the matter at hand, but this time she knew she had to bide her time and develop this relationship — or this deal was going to be a dead horse. She needed this woman on side, even if she had dinner booked in with the CEO for next week at her favourite restaurant — and was confident he would understand her value. Regardless, she still needed the budget from marketing to keep the billings coming in, and the budget lay with this woman.

With a sigh she headed back to her office, knowing she would be inundated with emails and requests for meetings the minute she walked back into the room.

Josephine had always loved her work. She had started as a speechwriter and had grown to be the CEO of an events business that focused exclusively on the highest level of leadership—CEOs, board members, chairmen and investors. She was considered brilliant with her skill set of positioning high-profile CEOs, developing their thought leadership focuses, and creating a public image that inspired high share prices and happy customers.

She had a tight staff of fifteen and billed more than $10 million a year in services and events—$500 000 of which she took home as a salary. Not to mention her considerable bonuses.

Josephine hadn't come from money, but she'd always wanted it—and she'd figured out very early on that the only way she was going to get it was to make it herself.

And, if she had to admit it, she did make money in a pretty spectacular fashion. The problem was she never held onto it for long. Sure, she'd been on some amazing trips around the world (okay, more than amazing—she had pretty much lived a five-star life in every continent on the planet) and she also had an incredible wardrobe. She owned enough designer clothes (especially business suits) to almost never wear the same jacket twice in a year. Her handbags were to-die-for, and she drove a convertible Aston Martin. She pretty much had everything she'd ever yearned for in her twenties.

Growing up in the upper North Shore in Sydney, she'd had a comfortable, middle-class life. She went to the local public high school—where she aced the communications subjects all the way through—and graduated university with honours. Her parents were both teachers, and she and her two brothers had always been taught the value of education. Her parents did not, however, value material things in the way Josephine did. They kept the same couch for 30 years, and their version of a home renovation was putting a tin roof on the porch of their three-bedroom brick veneer.

While she loved them dearly, she'd always secretly wondered whether she was adopted—that perhaps the Packers had accidentally left her at the hospital and her parents had picked her up by mistake. They'd paid for what she needed but, in Josephine's view, rarely for what she wanted. So she had spent the past 25 years working her way toward all those things she had dreamed about—and, she had to admit, she had now fulfilled most of her high school fantasies of beautiful things and lots of overseas travel.

Lately, however, these things didn't seem to give her the same thrill as they used to. The things she used to yearn for had become a given—not something to be celebrated. More than that, she found herself waking up at night, wondering what would happen if her biggest client stopped retaining her services, or whether her rent was too high in the swanky city offices she had moved into.

At 43 Josephine was, to the eyes of the outside world, a complete success. She was attractive, stylish, charming and driven, with more than her fair share of male attention and some close girlfriends as well. In fact, her best friend, Karen, had known her since she was thirteen years old and starting year 7. She was lucky enough to have the privilege of a best friend who knew her completely—without the misconceptions of what people saw when they looked at her today.

She had fallen in love deeply in high school and had her heart broken at university. While she had had many boyfriends since then, at various levels of seriousness, she had never married. 'The one who got away,' she often sighed to herself, especially when she heard a '90s love ballad and was transported back to those days.

Very few things had got away in her life since. She lived with purpose and a drive to always do more—go harder, build bigger—and she treated relationships the same way. Sometimes she dated very handsome, very attentive men — ones who usually had little in the way of finances, but big dreams. Her financial success meant she definitely held the power over them — no matter how attractive or masculine they appeared to be. But it was becoming predictably boring. She quickly lost respect for their choices and their neediness for the life she provided. These relationships never lasted long.

She'd then swing the other way and date successful, corporate leaders — men whose first priority was their work and who networked effortlessly at influential levels. These men could help her meet the kind of people who needed her work and what it could deliver. They were good for business. They saw her as a trophy.

These relationships never lasted too long either, and both kinds were exhausting in their own way. They each required her to be a particular version of herself — not the whole person — and sustaining this grew tiring.

She was rarely alone, but lately had started feeling lonely even when in a crowd. It secretly worried her. She had always known what she wanted — and ruthlessly went after it. Now, she wasn't so sure.

She had gotten herself into a position where she needed to push harder than ever with her work. She was highly leveraged with a portfolio of investment properties, all purchased through borrowing against her stunning renovated terrace in Paddington — which she had owned outright, but had now used as collateral.

She had a boutique vineyard in the Hunter Valley, in a syndicate with three others. She also had a penthouse apartment on the Gold Coast, an apartment in Chatswood and a renovated farmhouse/guesthouse in Bowral. All were doing incredibly well thanks to Airbnb. She rarely worried about the millions she owed the bank, because she knew her properties would more than likely pay themselves off over time — all she had to do was keep her ridiculously large income rolling through the door to make all the parts move.

Her business had generated her many 'bonuses' outside her salary, which helped fund her overseas travel and designer wardrobe. If she didn't keep billing, however, all these extras would have to stop. Everything came down to her winning the next deal, implementing the next event or having the next idea that could bring large licks of revenue to the table.

She knew she appeared to have it all, but lately Josephine felt as if a giant flat rock had been laid on her chest—gently pressing all the air out of her, as she struggled to keep her breath steady against the crushing burden of responsibility. All her life, she had gladly taken on responsibility—it was necessary to get to the next level, to get what she wanted. Lately, however, it was becoming more of a load. The money she had to generate to keep her incredible lifestyle going seemed that much harder to make. And if she was honest with herself, she was less naturally motivated than she used to be. In her twenties and thirties, running hard at what she wanted had come very naturally for her. In her forties, however, that run had become a brisk walk—with bouts of wanting to lie down.

She rarely told anyone these thoughts, however—doing so would completely ruin the image of herself she had so carefully constructed. Sometimes she complained to Karen that she was tired or stressed—and she knew Karen worried about her. But she also knew that Karen completely adored her, and was in awe of all she had achieved. She believed absolutely in her infallibility. This meant, while Josephine may worry about her future, Karen believed without a doubt that Josephine would succeed at pretty much everything she went for—based, of course, on the 30-year demonstration of exactly that.

There was only one thing that Josephine had ever wanted that she didn't get. And that was a man. Not just any man—Brad Malone, her year 12 sweetheart, who she had dated all the way to third-year uni, studying communications while he studied technology.

She had been sure they would end up together—by the time she was 20, everyone was always saying it was only a matter of time before Brad proposed. After university, however, Brad got an internship in a tech firm in Silicon Valley, and it was an opportunity too good to refuse—so the couple swore they would make a long-distance relationship work. And they had tried. But after a period of long phone calls and economy flights, Josephine heard less and less from Brad—till he finally told her over the phone that it was over. They were too far apart and he was in the throes of America's biggest tech boom. And so, the love of her life slipped through her fingers.

While Josephine was devastated at the time, she'd told herself she'd gotten over it. After all, she was attractive and ambitious, and many men were seeking her attention. But by her mid-thirties, she started to suspect she would never feel about anyone else the way she did about Brad. Karen knew this—which was why it was big news between them that Brad was coming to the reunion.

Josephine knew she still looked good—as well she should, with the amount she spent on face creams, hair extensions, regular facials and daily yoga. She continually invested in herself—this was part of her success at work, and with no children to worry about she had the time.

On some level, Josephine regretted never having children. The right time had never seemed to come, or the right person to have them with. In her uni years, she'd expected she would have kids with Brad. Since then, she'd always had something else to focus on. She adored Karen's kids, and spent loads on them as a benevolent and invested 'Aunt' figure. But she never committed deeply to anyone else. At 43, she had started to wonder whether her life would get lonelier as she got older.

Giving herself a shake and pushing that thought from her mind, Josephine finished her preparations for yet another dinner at a five-star restaurant with a client. She ate out at least five nights a week—and when she stayed home, usually ordered in sushi or Thai food from the restaurants down the road.

She knew she didn't want a late night—and she hoped her client would pull out his corporate card when the bill came. Letting his company pay was a whole lot less of a big deal than if it was coming out of his own pocket—like it did for her. The bill was rarely less than $300, and when you dined out as much as she did, Josie hoped someone else would pick up the tab at least half the time.

Tomorrow she would shop up a storm with Karen. The thought crossed her mind to take them both to the day spa at the Langham for facials and high tea—Karen would love that. She quickly sent her EA a text, asking her to see if any appointments were available.

She picked up her new Burberry bag, and coated her lips in Hollywood red lipstick. Even at 6.30 at night, she wanted to look fresh and at her best—her clients appreciated it, and they counted on her for their dose of glamour.

After ordering an Uber Black, she quickly Googled Brad Malone to see what had been said about him lately. At the top of the results were recent stories from *The New York Times* and *The Washington Post* about a speech Brad had given on alternative energy sources. Apparently, Brad's company had designed an algorithm for a new battery source that was giving Elon Musk's company a run for its money, and would mostly likely be bought by Musk in one of the larger mergers of the year.

Josephine's heart quickened as she looked at the pics of Brad. He was still so handsome—with a touch of grey in his hair. He had a great body, and looked fit and lean. His eyes looked a bit harder than when she knew him, but she understood what it must have taken for Brad to get to the level he had. His company was worth billions, and he had joined the ranks of billionaire just before his 40th birthday. He was a declared workaholic, and usually dating models or alternative type actresses. He had been married and divorced twice, and now seemed content to have a new girlfriend every 18 months. While plenty of news articles appeared about him, rarely was one an interview with him. He seemed to avoid the usual celebrity that went with money in the United States.

And now he was coming to their high school reunion. Josephine felt nervous and excited about this development—how much would he remember about their connection? She was glad she had invited Karen and Russ to stay with her—she would need Karen around as support and, of course, Russ was never far from Karen. She only hoped that Russ didn't insist on inviting Jasper. He was Russ's best buddy in high school—the good-natured jock, who partied hard and was always the last man standing at any event.

She knew the two of them still went fishing together, and had no doubt Jasper would love the free drinks and food that went with a night at her five-star hotel.

Jasper no longer amused her as he had in high school. He now annoyed her. Perennially a teenager in his mind, Jasper had never, in her view, grown up. He might buy the first round at the bar to make himself look good at the start, but he'd then rely on free drinks from everyone else for the rest of the night. At parties, he still drank to the point of drunk and then mouthed off at people randomly.

He didn't seem to stay in any job for too long, and usually picked up sales jobs where he could use his gift of the gab to charm people, at least for a while. But his party ways and lack of work ethic usually got him fired, and he was always scratching for money. None of this was something Josephine could respect from a person in their forties.

But Jasper was a minor concern compared to the much more interesting issue of Brad Malone. Seeing him again meant more to her than she cared to admit, even to herself.

# Chapter 5

# Jasper

The clock moved slowly toward 3 pm — too slowly for Jasper's liking. He was sitting in the showroom of his new job where he was supposed to be selling cars, both new and used. But nobody was in sight to sell to — and he was damned if he was going to go out and pace the lot like some of the old-time desperadoes. The only time Jasper did go out to the empty lot was to sneak in a cigarette. He knew all too well he was not supposed to be smoking out there, but if he went more than an hour without a cigarette, he felt agitated.

Smoking was a habit he'd picked up in high school and had never been able to kick. He had tried the gum, the patches and just quitting cold turkey, but none of it had stuck. He was smart enough to know the health risks — after all, who didn't? Rotting limbs, bulging eyes and warnings were plastered on every packet. But still, he kept smoking.

The one concession he did make was to move to roll-your-owns. These turned out to be more cost-effective than the $30 (and then some) packets he used to smoke — and for Jasper, anything that was cheaper was better.

He usually lived week to week — sometimes month to month when a job paid monthly. He hated those jobs, however, because he usually went through the bulk of his pay in the first ten days, and spent the rest of the month showing up at the pub for someone else's shout, and borrowing $50 off his mum.

He was hopeless with hanging onto money—it seemed to slip through his fingers like water. He never had enough, and Jasper had been thinking about this more lately. He was tired of scrounging. He had moved back into his mum's house last year, telling her she needed the company after his dad's death a few years back. In reality, Jasper needed the free rent. It was the only way he could afford to live and still have a life in Sydney—everything was so damn expensive.

So he moved back into his childhood room—with his trophies for sport and photos on the wall all around him. It sure was a turn-off when he brought women home, and he told many of them he was just visiting his mum and that he had his own place on the coast. This used to be true, until Jasper's lease had been terminated due to the constant late payment of his rent.

Jasper turned his mind to Jayne—someone he had gone to high school with. She'd been one of the prettier girls in high school with a great body, and she'd always been easy to talk to. He'd first seen her again earlier this week at the local IGA when his mum had sent him up there to replace the milk he had drunk straight from the carton—he was, after all, really thirsty.

\*\*\*

'Jayneeeee!' he cried in surprise when he saw her there. Her face was more lined and her body was not what it was when she was 18 but, at 43, she still looked pretty damn good. Jasper knew how to turn on the charm when he had to—he had been relying on that since puberty.

She turned towards him first in suspicion, but this quickly turned to happiness when she saw it was Jasper standing at the counter with his carton of milk. 'Oh my God, Jasper Weyland,' she said, and walked over and gave him a hug.

Jasper enjoyed this more than he cared to admit. It was so good to see someone from the good old days—when he was a sports god and could do no wrong.

'What's a nice girl like you doing in a place like this?' he drawled, enjoying her admiration. He knew he still looked pretty good—he hadn't let himself go and still had a head full of hair, although it was starting to get a little grey. So many of the guys he went to school with were now going bald, and it aged them incredibly. His dad had died with every hair still on his head, and Jasper was grateful for those genes.

He looked at Jayne's shopping in her basket and noticed it held school snacks and kids' shampoo. Disappointed, he realised of course someone like Jayne would have kids and a husband—she was way too good a catch to have stayed single. Jayne saw him staring at the basket and shrugged—she had nothing to be ashamed of, after all.

'Twins,' she said smiling at him and then looking back at the basket. Her girls were eight and seemed to be consuming more and more food every day. It was all Jayne could do to keep up with their increased appetites—and be grateful she didn't have boys to feed!

'Wow! I bet your husband is outnumbered,' Jasper commented, wondering whether she'd married someone from school. He hadn't heard from Russ or anyone else he still saw.

'I'm divorced, so the girls don't see their father too much,' Jayne replied.

*Divorced?* Jasper whistled in what he hoped was just his mind, and grinned broadly. This was his favourite type of woman—already with kids, no husband and likely to issue few demands on Jasper outside him providing his company and being nice to her kids.

'Sorry to hear that,' said Jasper, although in reality he was far from sorry. A shadow passed over Jayne's eyes, but she quickly recovered. 'Believe me, it's better this way,' she said breezily.

Jasper dug out the two dollars in twenty cent pieces he had taken from his mother's coin jar to pay for the milk and handed it over to the cashier.

'How about a catch-up?' he asked casually. 'I'm staying with Mum at the moment—Dad recently passed away, and she needs the company,' he quickly explained.

'Sure, I'd love to,' said Jayne, a little too quickly. Jasper's anti-commitment radar started to buzz, but he ignored it. Jayne Sampson had been one of his crushes in high school and he'd always regretted never going there.

Jasper was smart enough to not suggest dinner—he doubted Jayne would appreciate the fish and chips that his budget would allow—and went for an outing instead. 'I usually walk the dog for Mum every Saturday. How about we meet at London Park this weekend? You could bring the kids,' he said.

Jayne looked at him happily. She was thinking what a nice guy Jasper had turned out to be. Staying with his mum when his dad died, and thinking of her kids.

'You're on, but the girls stay with my mum and dad every second Saturday night, so it will just be me.'

Jasper gave her back a wide smile as they agreed to meet at 3 pm that Saturday, and then sauntered out of the shop. This had turned out to be a far better day than he could ever have imagined. As he walked home he thought he must remember to thank his mother for making him get the milk—who knew meeting Jayne again would come of it?

When he got home, he told his mum about seeing Jayne Sampson while buying milk.

'Yes, poor woman,' said his mother, shaking her head. His mum had lived in this area for more than 40 years, and not much went on that she didn't know about. Apparently she knew Jayne's mother well and they played bingo together at the local RSL.

'What do you mean?' asked Jasper, a little defensively.

'Apparently her husband became quite violent—and Jayne left him to keep those little girls safe,' said Jasper's mother. She enjoyed knowing everyone's business, and was quick to make moral judgements on who was in the right and the wrong. Having Jasper at home with her had proved to be a little embarrassing for her with her bingo friends. A few times he had come to the club to ask to borrow money, and she was sure some of her friends had heard. She had always solved Jasper's problems by buying him out of them, and now he had come to rely on it. It was proving impossible to change the habit of a lifetime.

'Never ask me in front of people,' she'd told Jasper several times. She loved her son and would do anything for her only child, but she knew in her heart Jasper was lazy. If she was completely honest with herself, she also knew he was using her for free rent. She chose to overlook this and pretend otherwise because it was nice to have the company since Jim had died. He was also handy at mowing the lawn and taking the rubbish out. She could have hired someone to do both jobs for far less than Jasper was costing her, but family was family.

Jasper processed the news of Jayne's divorce—a violent husband? *What a bastard*, he thought indignantly. Jasper was many things, but he would never hurt a woman, and despised men who did.

'I'm meeting up with her at the park on Saturday, when I take Winkle for his weekend walk,' Jasper informed his mother. He didn't usually tell her what his social plans were, but he was in a good mood and feeling close to his mother.

'Be careful there, Jasper,' his mother warned. 'She has had her heart broken badly. The last thing she needs is someone else moving in for a good time.'

Jasper instantly felt annoyed that he had confided in his mother about this. After all, he was a grown man and he didn't need that kind of advice or warning from her.

'Thanks for the vote of confidence, Mum,' he said, before grabbing the car keys and walking to the door. Another perk of living with his mother was using her car, meaning he didn't have to worry about paying one off himself.

He quickly departed before she could say anything else to annoy him, and headed to the pub for his evening beer. He always knew someone there who was up for a chat and a beer.

***

Back in the showroom, it was Saturday afternoon and Jasper's phone buzzed, dragging him back to his job and the long hours till 3 pm. He looked down and saw a text from Russ.

'Reunion looking good. Josephine has suite in the city — come hang with me and help me escape the girls!'

This whole week was turning out to be a good one. Jasper smiled as he responded with a thumbs up to Russ. He knew the reunion would be a chance for a good time. Of course, he was going to have to dodge questions around what he did now and who he lived with — after all, he had been expected to be a star athlete who made a name for himself in football, rather than a 43-year-old car salesman living with his mum.

But for now, he forgot about his current circumstances. He had a date with Jayne Sampson later today, and a free night out coming up for the reunion. Things were definitely looking up.

# Chapter 6

# Jayne

'What a blast from the past!' Jayne smiled to herself as she walked home from the supermarket. She couldn't believe she had bumped into Jasper after all these years. He looked good—although Jayne had to admit that most men looked good to her nowadays. It had been 18 months since she'd divorced Nick, and certainly no good male companionship had occurred before or since then.

Jayne sighed, as her mind briefly touched on Nick again. Divorcing him had been both traumatic and cathartic. She had put up with his erratic behaviour for about seven of their ten years of marriage, but it had started to get worse in the last couple of years—to the point where Jayne had become afraid of how he might hurt her physically. If Jayne had been on her own, she may have put up with it for longer to avoid being alone and accepting that her marriage was a failure. But she had two little girls to consider, and they were of an age where they modelled themselves on her.

Jayne thought happily about her girls who, at eight, were now thriving after the initial meltdown of the divorce. Her parents had been a huge help in providing stability for the girls, and Nick had actually been shocked enough when Jayne had the courage to leave him that he'd made some effort to spend time with them. He was still their father—or at least his version of a father.

Nick earned good money as a real estate agent for the lower North Shore, and he was great at being charming and always on call—which was what contributed to him being a total nightmare as a husband. He was always busy, always working weekends and never around. And when he was around, he wanted to relax, drink whisky and hear as little as possible from the girls.

At home he was short-tempered and hard to please—something which Jayne could accept at first, as she juggled her job at a law firm along with being a full-time mother and wife. But when Nick began to vent his frustration by shoving her, pushing her down to the ground and kicking her, she drew the line.

Sometimes she could not believe this was her life. She had always planned things so well. She was the in-house counsel for a large law firm—which meant that, rather than taking clients, the law firm was her client—and she did well. She wrangled the arrogant, entitled lawyers easily, and usually got her way in a corporate disagreement.

Her home life, however, was the complete opposite. With Nick, it was always about him, the demands of his job and the pressure he felt. Between that and the full-time job of looking after twin girls and the increasing demands of their schooling, she felt out of control and never in charge.

Leaving Nick 18 months ago had cleared a lot of chaos in her life. She no longer needed to avoid mood swings and dark tempers at home. However, a whole bunch of other considerations had come into play once she became a single mother.

While Nick contributed to the girls' upkeep, his payments of $2000 per month were nowhere near enough to cover costs for the girls. While they attended the local primary school, which was a good quality public school, the cost of all their extra-curricular activities and after-school care took a large bulk of that cash. Everything else Jayne had to pay for—like clothes, food and holidays.

Jayne earned $90 000 in her job and would have been able to make more, but she had negotiated diminished hours so she could be there to drop the girls to school and pick them up by 6 pm from after-school care. Law was a time-intensive career, and she was putting in the bare minimum of time in the office to still keep her in the game. She worked twice as fast as any other lawyer in the firm, and often sat up late at night, writing and planning so her workdays ran smoothly.

She earned super on top of her salary, but she was smart enough to know that 9.5 per cent of $90 000 was never going to add up to enough for her to retire on. But she had little other choice—the cost of bringing up the girls meant she never had enough spare to commit to savings.

Jayne realised she needed to do something about her financial position. But she was so busy keeping her head above water, and keeping the girls' lives running smoothly, that she never quite knew what that something was. They had sold their house after the divorce and Jayne had moved into a two-bedroom rental apartment near her parents' house. What money they'd received from the sale of the house had gone straight into paying back debt.

Nick had a taste for nice cars, insisting real estate agents needed to look successful—and he'd also invested in some dubious business ideas that did not pay off. So Jayne had gone from having a mortgage to pay off and debts to juggle, to just paying rent.

She tried, as always, to look on the bright side. While she had no savings to fall back on, she also didn't have crippling debt to add to her anxiety or a husband who kept adding to it. Of course, she knew this also meant that the possibility of her getting back into the property market was zero, at least in Sydney.

Jayne's parents had lived in their family home for more than 40 years. She knew it must be worth over $1.5 million now and that she would eventually inherit it. But Mum and Dad were in good health, and only in their late sixties, so it could be another 25 years before that happened—and they had to pay for aged care too. While Jayne didn't want to think about her parents dying, somewhere in the back of her mind, she knew that the only way she would ever own property again, outside of marrying someone who had some, was from any windfall she had from her parents.

Jayne idly wondered what Jasper's financial position was. He was living with his mother, which wasn't a great sign, but he did say that was to help after his dad died. One thing Jayne had learned was that you could no longer rely on romance or attraction to form a successful relationship. Money was important and, as her parents kept drilling into her, it was as easy to fall in love with a rich man as it was a poor one.

She had often wondered whether she would meet anyone again. She didn't enjoy being alone. While she was relieved to be free of her troubled marriage, she didn't want to spend her life as a single mother, with just her work and her kids to keep her company. She wanted more for herself. She wanted to be loved, and to love someone. To cuddle on the couch on a Friday night, and go away on the occasional romantic weekend.

Although she had failed at love the first time around, she still had hopes of a successful marriage, and of her own happily ever after. While it was too early to tell, Jasper might be someone she could see herself with. She looked forward to their meeting at the park, and also wondered if he was going to the reunion. She had been going back and forth in her head about even going herself. Turning up as a single mother was hardly a triumphant return.

She took a deep breath and decided, then and there, if Jasper was going, she would too. She needed some fun in her life and a night out with him would be just the ticket.

# Chapter 7

# **Brad**

'You've got two minutes to get to the boardroom, Brad,' said his assistant Rachel from the door of his office. She managed to deliver this kind of information in her casual Aussie accent that was never panicked, but always firm enough to know he had to listen.

She had been his EA for more than 15 years, and Rachel knew his whole life—or at least where he was supposed be, when and why—much better than he did. In a world of American attitudes and voices, it was great to have a slice of home in Rachel, looking after him like she did.

She had two small sons of her own and a husband—and she ran their lives with the same military precision with which she ran Brad's.

'Gotcha,' he said, closing his laptop and taking off his reading glasses. He had only just got them this year, and he alternated between feeling so old that he needed them and grateful that he could actually read without his eyes burning like fire, which they had been doing for months.

He'd put the sensation down to screen exhaustion, since he was looking at a screen for at least 12 hours a day—between research, reading and emails, and the hours he spent at night researching and reading for pleasure, his eyes were constantly exposed to a screen. It was only when Rachel insisted he see an optometrist that he realised his eyes needed glasses — and probably had for the past year or two.

This was not unusual for Brad — not paying attention to the everyday things was how he operated. His mind was always on the big picture, which was why Rachel had new suits delivered to his home every quarter and he had a housekeeper to run his household, as well as his other domestic staff — the gardener, pool guy, handyman and everyone else who came with an estate the size of his.

Brad counted once how many people it took to run his home and his life — it came to seven. That was a lot, he conceded. But it did free him up to look after the business, which to him was number one.

Since winning an internship in Silicon Valley after university, Brad had spent the past 20 years working. But it wasn't just work; it was an obsession. He had developed a tech business that used algorithms that could increase efficiency in pretty much every industry, and he had become renowned for innovation. There was no limit to the number of high-end people who worked with his product — including, most recently, his major deal with Elon Musk.

The news had sent his share price skyrocketing, and added millions to his net worth on paper. Brad had stopped caring about that a long time ago. Once you were officially announced a billionaire, the millions going up and down didn't mean much. He wasn't driven by the money, but by the challenge of growth — of innovating more, and creating something that nobody else had. In fact, lately Brad had felt like that was the only thing that mattered to him; that he was a function of his work and nothing else. And, if he was honest with himself, he wasn't sure he liked that feeling.

Relationships were complicated and annoyingly human, however. They meant there was someone else to please — somebody who demanded his time away from his work. While that first flush of attraction and excitement in a relationship always started well, it usually ended the same—with Brad becoming distant and avoiding calls, and then usually with Rachel breaking the news to the latest girlfriend that it wasn't going to work out.

While he did feel bad that Rachel delivered the message, he just didn't feel comfortable with emotional scenes. They made him feel awkward, and he never knew the right thing to say. So he said nothing, and avoided emotional trauma altogether.

Brad was no monk. His girlfriends were women who would make most men's jaws hit the floor. He had dated models, actresses, heiresses, bohemian beauties—you name it, Brad could get it. The mixture of his incredible wealth and good looks meant few women were invulnerable to his charms. At 43, he was physically at his peak and still swam kilometres every day—a throwback to the swimming meets he used to train for as a kid.

Brad's parents had pushed him hard as a kid—whether in the academic arena or athletics, they had expected him to be the best. They had scheduled his life to the point where he put enough time into each of these activities, every day, to become the best. The feeling of winning Brad got from this as a kid was echoed hollowly by the feeling he got today when he had a business win, or played tennis against a friend and flogged them on the court. Today, Brad realised, he didn't care so much about the winning, but he sure didn't want to lose.

These feelings made it harder and harder to find pleasure in things, in people, or in achievements. All he was compelled to do was push harder, work harder, and avoid losing.

Brad sat in his boardroom, listening idly to his head of finance talk about operation expansion plans, and how the budget had blown out by 20 per cent on the build in his new London offices.

'Make cuts and get it back to the number we all agreed on,' said Brad, after a 20-minute explanation on why the budget had been blown, and how things were underestimated in the first place.

His head of finance squirmed. Colin knew it would come to this and he hated to be the one to deliver bad news. Brad never screamed or shouted, but his cold analysis of any situation and his almost robot-like assessments left Colin terrified of losing his job.

It was now obvious that the $20 million overrun was not going to be accepted. Colin, who knew Brad well, had guessed this before he'd even entered the room. But he'd foolishly hoped that the share price movement would have made Brad a little more forgiving today, enough to let the over budget ride.

'Either pull in the overspend, or sack whoever is running the London operation,' said Brad unemotionally before standing up to leave. This meeting was over. Colin continued to blabber about deals with Richard Branson that were in play, and that the UK head would be instrumental in their global growth plan.

'Anyone who can spend $20 million of my money without approval is not someone I can rely on,' said Brad, and with that he left the room, leaving Colin to deal with the problem.

Brad knew Colin would deal with it. He had been running the finance side of Brad's business for more than 10 years, and was used to pulling rabbits out of hats. Lately, however, Brad had noticed Colin slowing down. Getting into work at 8.30 am, not 6.30, and not responding to Brad's midnight emails until the next day.

Brad suspected Colin was burning out, and that was something he had little respect for. If people couldn't run at his pace, they shouldn't be there. His was not your regular 9-to-5 business, and people had gotten very rich from working for him. Brad had never minded people making money—but he did expect them to give 150 per cent of their efforts in return.

He would use this UK issue as a test for Colin—and if he didn't pull the overspend back, Brad would appoint a global head of finance over Colin. He'd find someone younger and hungrier, who wanted to make serious money—the kind of money only someone like Brad could pay, to hire the best.

When Brad got back to his office, Rachel was just hanging up the phone. 'Your Sydney trip is all organised,' she said with her usual efficiency. Brad instantly felt annoyed. That damn school reunion. His mother had been leaving messages and nagging Rachel for months for him to attend. She would, of course, use it as an occasion to show him and his achievements off as her own when he returned—which was why he rarely did return. As soon as Brad could escape from the overbearing, high-expectation parents he called his own, he did.

Of course, he had looked after them. He would have to be a complete bastard not to share the incredible wealth he had amassed with his family. He had bought his parents a harbourside house in Mosman, and his younger brother a penthouse in the city. He sent them on great holidays, organised by Rachel, and provided huge presents for birthdays and Christmases (also organised by Rachel, who was fantastic at that kind of thing). The only thing he did not give them was time.

His time was precious, and his parents had taken enough of it when he was a kid. They'd pushed him harder than any other kid at school had been, training him to be a winner from birth. They didn't care about the parties he missed or the stress he felt; they were determined to make him a champion. Well, they got what they wanted, but in the process he lost all affection for his family. He knew they were a big part of the reason he had been able to climb the heights he had—but also why he was emotionally shut off and exhausted.

But there was no getting out of this reunion. His mother had booked it into his diary with Rachel 18 months earlier, and rang weekly to remind him. Of course, Rachel took those calls too.

So he was going to spend an awkward night with people he hadn't seen in more than 25 years. *Great*, he thought grimly, as he mentally prepared for all that a trip to Sydney would entail.

He was curious to see one person, however. In fact, if he was honest with himself, the thought that he might see her again was the thing that tipped the decision into a yes.

He had not heard from Josie in years—a few months after he stopped returning her calls. He knew then that he wasn't ready for a long-term commitment. He wanted to prove himself at work—and he had done that on a grand scale. But, occasionally, he heard someone laugh, or smelt apple shampoo on a woman, and he was reminded of her—and it always made him smile.

Brad wondered idly what Josie was like now as he readied himself to leave for the airport. He was taking his own jet, so he didn't have to worry about security and the usual process of commercial airlines—nothing but the best for Brad Malone.

# Chapter 8

# **Memory lane**

Ben Jamieson was looking forward to the school reunion — there would only be few friends there who he didn't catch up with already. Staying in Sydney meant he'd kept many of the friends he had at school — none of the cool kids, like Brad or Jasper, but they were good guys who had always appreciated a laugh and some good old-fashioned male bonding.

Ben was going to the reunion out of pure curiosity. His interest was part of his profession really. He was a financial planner and had built a successful firm in eastern Sydney. His clients ranged from CEOs to trust fund kids, and he had pretty much seen everything in the past 20 years. Money did curious things to people, and Ben usually had a front row seat to see it all.

He had the (some might say annoying) habit of assessing everyone's personality in relation to what they earned. It was like a hobby for him, and a way to keep his sense of intuition about people sharp. He always did the work with the client and made sure he designed financial strategies just for them. But he also knew his instinct around people made him extremely insightful about their true situation.

The reunion was going to be pure gold for seeing what had become of those he had gone to high school with. He had even heard that Brad Malone was coming — a bona fide billionaire now.

Ben whistled to himself as he thought about the night—it was going to be a good one. He was sure to be kept busy observing the behaviour of people he'd had nothing in common with 20 years ago. If nothing else, he was hoping to confirm his predictions about how people would end up—many of which he had written in his high school year book. It occurred to him to find the book now, to remind himself of those names and faces he would be seeing again for the first time in a long time. A trip down memory lane was just what he needed.

***

Meanwhile, Karen and Josie were shopping up a storm. Despite knowing she couldn't afford a single scarf inside, Karen loved going into all the shiny, bare stores that Josie shopped in—where the racks only had about six items hanging on them, like each one was a piece of art.

'OMG, check this out!' Josie giggled, holding up a leopard skin scrap of material that apparently went with a Dolce & Gabbana scarf set. 'A matching G-string!"

Karen laughed as Josie waved the piece of lace triumphantly, thinking of what a horrifying sight it would be to see herself in it. 'Only $700,' joked Josie as she put it back. While she did spend money, she wasn't stupid, and that was an insane price for underwear.

Karen loved touching all the gorgeous fabrics, and with Josie around, none of the snooty sales women hassled her. They all knew Josie was a spender, and were waiting silently by for a chance to hard sell when the time was right.

And Josie didn't disappoint. She tried on at least ten things, and bought half of them.

'You just dropped $7000!' Karen whispered to Josie, who had handed over her platinum card.

'It's a business expense—I need to look the part,' shrugged Josie, with very little reaction at all to the amount of money she had just spent. After all, people paid for her image and she had to keep it up to date. Grooming and wardrobe was one of her bigger line items—added up over the past ten years, the amount she'd spent in this area could have bought an apartment. Josie sometimes felt a twinge when she looked at the end of year numbers, but refused to stop buying at least some of the latest designer styles. She was at the top of her game, and needed to stay that way in the eyes of the business community. Clothes, shoes and bags sure helped with this.

Karen felt envious again, thinking of the white bohemian-gypsy dress Bella had found for her online. It was $120 from ASOS, and she was counting on it arriving on time. While it was a good find for the money, it would never compete with Josie's designer threads. She found herself sucking in her stomach and straightening her shoulders just being in these shops. She certainly never considered she would get to wear any of the items hanging so sparsely on the racks, and being around them made her feel, well, inferior.

'Let's grab lunch,' said Josie, instantly cheering Karen up. A glass of chardy and an expensive salad would do just the trick—more chardonnay and less salad, that is. And usually chips went with the lunch to make it all worthwhile.

Meanwhile, food was the furthest thing from Josie's mind. Her focus was back on Brad. What was he like now? Did he ever think about her? Why was he coming back? He didn't have a girlfriend at the moment, from what she could ascertain from the gossip pages, but she knew all too well that those pages were only half the story. He may well have a dozen women on the side, with his money and power keeping quiet.

Thinking about Brad was proving to be a pleasant diversion from thinking about work. The constant thought and worry she put into her business was exhausting. While she had achieved great things, the level of pressure on her day to day meant she always had something to think about, solve and create. What used to be challenges that motivated her had now turned into pressures she found it hard to escape from. The pleasant diversion of Brad Malone and the reunion was appreciated.

Karen knew from the wistful look on her face that Josie was thinking about Brad. Karen hadn't seen Josie look like that in a long time — too long, in fact. While she often envied her friend and the money and incredible lifestyle she'd worked for, she also knew she wouldn't trade the life she had with Russ and the kids for it. Josie must be lonely, and Karen hoped that Brad Malone and the reunion turned into something positive for Josie — she could sense her friend needed a change.

'What's our game plan?' asked Karen after taking a large sip of her wine. She knew Josie would want to plan this reunion in detail.

Josie smiled slyly. 'Well, dahling,' she drawled, 'it's all about making an entrance.'

Karen laughed. This was going to be fun.

# Chapter 9

# **Reunited**

Reunion day had finally arrived—and those going had mixed feelings. Russ was looking forward to letting his hair down and having a few drinks. Jasper was looking forward to a lot of drinks and a possible interlude with Jayne. Karen was nervous about what people would think of her now—would they think she had gotten fat? Josie was obsessing about seeing Brad and whether they would feel any connection at all. And Jayne hoped that Jasper would single her out. Their dog walk had gone well—and she needed some romance. Brad, on the other hand, was dreading it all—except, of course, for seeing Josephine, if only to prove to himself that work really was his only love.

Ben Jamieson was already mentally calculating the odds on people actually achieving his year book predictions from 25 years ago.

Getting ready was also a mixed affair. Josie had decided that Karen should get dressed with her, which meant her make-up artist could also do her hair and face. This was, as usual with Josie, incredibly generous and Karen appreciated it. The two of them sat in Josie's enormous three-bedroom suite, getting pampered in a way that was normal for Josie and a real treat for Karen.

Josie was also getting more hair extensions put in. Her hair had been falling out in a worrying fashion of late and she needed a bit more volume. 'Damn! I'm going to be bald soon,' she complained to Karen as her makeup artist of ten years artfully hid all the bare patches. Karen could not help but giggle. Josie would still look stunning bald but, of course, that was not going to be any consolation right now. The hair extensions, however, were a thick, glossy chestnut, and the end result was entirely gorgeous.

Karen was pretty happy with how she looked too. Her long blonde hair was in soft curls that trailed all the way down her back. Her make-up made her face more defined, and her blue eyes bigger. She knew Russ would like it and, she had to admit, she liked it herself. She and Josie would make a great entrance at the reunion, and having her best friend at her side 25 years after school ended felt good. It was something to be proud of.

As Josie was getting dressed, Karen heard a knock at the door. Still in her hotel robe, she opened it to find Russ standing there, grinning from ear to ear, with Jasper behind him.

'Babe!' Russ exclaimed, grabbing Karen around the waist and spinning her around. 'You look gorgeous!'

Karen laughed as she kissed her husband, and then smiled and greeted Jasper.

Jasper watched the couple affectionately. For so long he'd felt that Russ had settled down too early, missing his chance to have a good time and sow his wild oats. When he watched Karen and Russ together now, however, he realised how lucky they were. They had found each other young and built a life together. They were still in love and, Jasper had to admit, he felt a little jealous of his old friend.

To break the moment, Jasper gave a wolf-like howl—and yelled, 'Let's get this party started.' To him, of course, this meant drinks. Karen gave him a stern look. 'No getting loaded before we even get there, Jasper,' she said in her best 'Mum' tone. Jasper pretended to look offended, as he quickly hunted for the mini bar in the room. Finding a bottle of Veuve chilling in an ice bucket, he approvingly held it up for inspection. 'Josephine always had great taste,' he said.

Just then, Josie came out of her room. She was dressed in an emerald-green cocktail dress with a black-lace back, and real emerald earrings. She looked for all the world like a movie star and everyone, including Karen, gasped at the sight of her. 'Tongues back in boys,' she said in a vampire fashion, before bursting out laughing. Karen clapped and walked all the way around her. 'OMG, Brad Malone is not going to know what hit him,' she said excitedly, taking in the incredible sight that was her best friend.

'That tosser!' snorted Jasper, as the champagne cork popped. 'Who cares what he thinks?'

Josie rolled her eyes but held her tongue. Why cause an argument this early in the night? She'd known Russ would invite Jasper, and Karen was so excited about the whole hotel thing that she didn't want to ruin it for her.

'I'm going to get my dress on!' squeaked Karen, running into her room, while Jasper poured four glasses of champagne right to the brim.

*Why not?* thought Josie, grateful for the Dutch courage. She took a very long sip.

***

Meanwhile, Jayne was giving her parents last-minute instructions on what the girls could watch on Netflix. 'Kids channel only, Mum,' she yelled from her bedroom, while tonging her hair with the GHD. She knew her parents were hopeless with any sort of tech, and the girls usually tricked them into watching things that were not appropriate for their age.

She looked at herself critically in the mirror. 'Not bad,' she admitted. The fake tan she'd been rubbing on herself for days had given her a healthy glow. Her black velvet dress was short, and showed off legs that were still athletic and toned. She wore more make-up than usual, but had done a half-decent job of it. This was going to be as good as it got—and she hoped it was enough to keep Jasper's attention.

While she was dreading seeing all the couples while she was single, she also knew she wouldn't be the only divorced woman there. By her age, a lot of women had found themselves single again, and many of them at the reunion would have their eyes out for their next relationship. Finding a man in this city was like looking for hen's teeth, and she may well have competition for Jasper's attention tonight. Thinking of this, she adjusted her push-up bra and gave herself a little more cleavage. After all, it was a jungle out there.

*** 

Brad Malone stared out the window of his Sydney penthouse apartment. While he rarely came here, he still kept his own apartment at Circular Quay. It had all the clothes he would need, and was stocked up with everything imaginable. Even he had to admit this city was beautiful, but he watched the people milling about below dispassionately.

Thank God he'd seen his parents briefly yesterday, so he didn't have to deal with them today. His mother looked older, he'd noticed, and had clung to him in a way that was more desperate, more needy, than ever. He had done his duty and given her his full attention. She was his mother, after all, no matter what sort of tyrant she had been growing up.

He'd almost felt sorry for her, until she'd reminded him that the local paper was going to be covering the reunion and she'd let them know he was home for it. Typical of his mother to ensure she didn't miss a chance to promote her pride and joy. Brad had been dodging the press for years now, and the local North Shore rag was not where he wanted to be spending his time.

He made his way downstairs from the penthouse in his private lift. He had a driver picking him up to take him to the reunion, held at their old school — hardly glamorous — with an after-party at a city hotel. His Tom Ford suit would look out of place in the school hall, but his mother had told him the dress code was 'cocktail'. 'Let's get on with it,' he muttered to himself, as he stepped off the curb and into the waiting car.

\*\*\*

Ben Jamieson was already there. He had been part of the volunteer committee to help put the reunion together and was now helping set up. The hall looked pretty good—one of the women had come up with the theme of 'movie classics'—and the hall was covered in posters from movies from their formative years. *The Breakfast Club, St. Elmo's Fire, Wall Street, Pretty in Pink, The Lost Boys.* The room kind of resembled an old Video Ezy and that, combined with the streamers thrown around, gave it a festive feel. Ben cracked a beer and positioned himself at the front where names were to be marked off. He was looking forward to this.

\*\*\*

Jayne got out of the taxi and walked up to the hall. She didn't want to be first, and luckily a queue of people were waiting to get in. *OMG, that's Kylie from home economics class. She is HUGE,* Jayne thought gleefully, and then smiled in her direction. 'Hi Jayne,' gushed Kylie, before starting to blather on about what she had been doing for the past 25 years. It made total sense that she had become a pastry chef; she certainly was a product of her profession.

It wasn't until Kylie introduced her husband that Jayne started to feel worried. So Kylie had managed to stay married.

'Where's your hubby?' Kylie asked. Jayne was tempted to lie and say he couldn't make it. Instead, she said evenly, 'I've been divorced for 18 months now.' Jayne could see the glee on Kylie's face when she delivered the news. *While I may be fat,* she seemed to be thinking, *at least I still have a husband in tow.* Jayne gave her most winning smile to them both and headed over to tick her name off the list. She saw Ben Jamieson standing at the door. He was someone she was genuinely pleased to see.

'Hi Ben,' she smiled, leaning in to give him a kiss. Ben had been one of the good guys at school. Not someone she would have dated, but someone decent whom she trusted.

'Looking great, Jayne,' he said appreciatively, and she felt better. Not everyone was going to judge her for being single.

She stood talking to Ben for a while, scanning inside the hall for Jasper at the same time. Finding the room empty of anyone interesting, she glanced outside at the registration desk and almost gasped out loud. Josephine was there with Karen, Russ and Jasper, looking absolutely drop-dead gorgeous and for all the world like part of the foursome. Jayne felt a sinking sensation in her stomach. She couldn't compete with Josephine. If she wanted Jasper, she would have him.

Just as she was thinking about that, Jasper caught her eye and winked. He made the hand motion of one minute and then registered his name before walking straight over to her and whistling softly. 'You look incredible,' he said appreciatively, and Jayne's heart beat faster. While she was no competition for Josephine, she suddenly felt confident. Jasper had made it clear he was interested in her, and that was exactly what Jayne had hoped for.

Josephine was whispering in Karen's ear, while Russ chatted casually to Ben. It was then Jayne remembered she'd read Brad Malone was coming. No wonder Josephine was not interested in Jasper. Jayne knew Josephine and Brad had been an item in high school and it didn't look like Josephine had a wedding ring on. Jayne guessed that Brad would be Josie's target for the night.

The thought gave her confidence. Grabbing Jasper's hand, she went over to Karen and Josie and gave them both a hug. They both looked happy to see her, if a bit surprised at the fact she was holding Jasper's hand. She stood there chatting happily, catching up on the past 25 years, and realised the night was going to be great. While life was so different now from how it was in high school, she understood these people. When you've seen someone with pimples and bad hair, coping with heartbreak and algebra, you know them in a way that you can't possibly know other adults. *History is a beautiful thing*, Jayne thought happily.

Just then, every head in the room turned at the same time. Brad Malone had walked in and he looked, well, hot. Josie took a sharp intake of breath and grabbed Karen's arm, almost to the point of her nails drawing blood. Instead of yelping in pain, Karen laughed out loud, as if Josephine had said the funniest thing she had heard all year. This was enough to break the tension, and Josie looked at her and laughed too. That's the thing about best friends. They always knew what to do in a time of need.

Brad looked up and saw Josephine laughing. *God, she was still beautiful*, he thought to himself, and felt a pang of something he had not felt in years. This in itself scared him. He wasn't used to feeling foreign emotions — it made him feel out of control, and he was always in control.

Nodding tightly at her, he made his way over to Ben and Russ and shook their hands. These were good guys, and Brad was happy to take his attention away from Josephine.

The rest of the room, of course, was whispering behind their hands about Brad. What was it about making billions of dollars that made everyone else in awe of you? Brad knew, of course, that money was the ultimate score card and, while he wasn't motivated by it in itself anymore, he was more than aware of the power it had over people in general. Money made you superior, and even though he didn't make that direct a connection, his general behaviour gave off superiority most of the time. Mostly that was because he was quiet and aloof. He was usually thinking about work and distracted around people. This gave people the perception that he wasn't quite with them, and most likely too important and successful to be giving them his attention.

Brad knew this to be caused by a level of social awkwardness — he had never been good in crowds and words didn't flow off his tongue easily. Hiding behind who he was and what he'd achieved proved to be convenient a lot of the time. Ben Jamieson, on the other hand, chatted easily to Brad—about his work, what tech he was working on and how often he came back home. While Ben chatted, Russ headed in Karen's direction. 'Come and say hi, you guys,' he said firmly, after having been briefed by his wife that Josephine was still interested in Brad.

He kissed Jayne on the cheek, noting how close she was standing to Jasper, and hoped that his friend didn't muck her around. She had always been a nice girl and he'd heard she had gotten divorced recently.

He grabbed Karen's hand and pulled her over to Brad. Karen, of course, grabbed Josie's, and they went together like a chain of paper dolls. Jasper grabbed Jayne and went over too—he wanted to see what all the fuss was about.

Josie's heart was pounding so loud she was worried Brad would hear it. Brad looked up to see the group coming toward him. His eyes found Josie's and looked piercingly at her. She stared back, and as everyone moved forward, their eyes did not break their gaze.

'Josie,' Brad said softly, while continuing to look into her eyes. 'Brad,' she mouthed breathlessly. Everyone else stood around awkwardly, feeling the electricity between the two of them—which was broken, of course, by Jasper.

'Whose shout?' he cried, looking towards the makeshift bar the committee had set up. Typical Jasper, but it also eased the tension and everyone laughed.

'I see nothing has changed, mate,' laughed Brad, shaking Jasper's hand. He felt his accent becoming more Australian again and, as everyone stood around catching up, Brad felt more relaxed and more himself than he had in a while.

Jasper went to get the first round of drinks (as per usual), and Jayne went with him to help carry them. Karen stood with Russ's arm around her waist, talking with her best friend and the billionaire.

Ben Jamieson watched all this with interest. In his brief chat with Brad, he had found him to be serious but decent. He knew working out what really motivated everyone around him must be tough—when you had that kind of money, you always had to doubt what was real. He saw it a lot with his financial planning clients who had money—especially those who came from family money and so were almost born wary.

Self-made people were a little different, and usually got burned a few times and had to learn the hard way. Brad seemed to be self-contained and quiet. Ben was looking forward to seeing the night's proceedings unfold, in particular the tension between Josephine and Brad. She was a stunning woman—it was almost hard to believe someone as elegant as she was had come from this school. But Ben sensed she was not particularly happy. She had the air of someone who had everything she ever wanted—and was still searching. Maybe she would find it tonight, Ben thought happily. He always wanted to see everyone get their happy ending.

Karen was telling the group about their children, and Russ chimed in occasionally with parts of the story he felt Karen was forgetting. Brad listened intently and, for the first time, felt a twinge of jealousy at what was obviously a very happily married couple. He had never had children, never found the right person or had the time, but from the obvious pride in the voices of the couple before him, he realised he had missed out on a lot of joy.

Josie also chimed in about the kids at times. She was their godmother, and adored buying them things and taking Bella to over the top places. Brad enjoyed the enthusiasm in Josephine's voice as she talked of them, and asked her whether she had her own kids. The silence was deafening as Josie shook her head quickly.

Karen quickly piped up. 'Josie has been too busy building her empire. I've been loaning her mine, which has turned her off,' she laughed. Josie smiled gracefully in her direction, and spoke briefly about her business and who her clients were.

Brad was impressed. He knew many of her clients, and had seen the work she had done with them. Josie had obviously made money and built her own success. Brad was incredibly relieved. Someone who didn't need money was usually who he went for. Those who didn't have it always ended up becoming needy and, well, he had to admit, weak.

He continued to ask Josie questions about her work and, as they got further and further into conversation, Karen and Russ drifted away, catching up with old classmates and comparing notes.

Jasper brought back the drinks and then he and Jayne also started working the room together.

'I hope this one's the right one for Jasper,' Karen whispered to Russ. That's what Russ loved about his wife. Instead of thinking the way he did—that Jasper would blow it—she looked at the upside and hoped Jasper would find love.

'Well, it would be a good match,' said Russ as he watched Jasper and Jayne laughing together.

They heard the screech of a microphone being turned on and their old school captain, Jodie Field, come on stage.

'Welcome, class of 1992!' she yelled into the microphone as everyone cheered. 'Tonight we are going to party!' With that, Vanilla Ice came through the PA, and the crowd started dancing badly to 'Ice Ice Baby' and other such cheesy hits from their teenage years.

Brad very quickly realised he was not going to be one of the dancing crowd. 'Let's get out of here,' he grinned at Josie and, grabbing her hand, pulled her out the side exit.

They both laughed like they were cutting class as they raced through the quadrangle and past classrooms that didn't look too much different from their era.

# Chapter 10

# The gathering

'I can't believe it's been 25 years since we were here,' said Josie with wonder as she looked fondly at the library, a place where she had spent a lot of her time. She also remembered how simple life had been then. The troubles she'd thought she had were so minor. And her dreams were so bright, and so out there in the future for her to chase.

Brad watched her profile, and thought how beautiful she was — a different kind of beauty from when they were at school, more ethereal and womanly. He liked the tiny laugh lines at the corners of her mouth, and the way her eyes crinkled when she smiled. She had aged extremely well.

They found themselves at the school gym, somewhere they had spent a lot of time together in year 12. Josie would watch Brad play basketball and they had often made out behind the stands. 'Let's hang out in the gym,' said Brad, pulling Josie toward the double doors.

'I think it's locked up,' said Josie, noting the new double bolt system on the doors.

With a sly smile, Brad pulled her to the side of the building and through a door clearly signposted as the boys' bathrooms. He turned the fluoro lights on and led her to the back of the room and a door marked Cleaner. From there, they walked into a broom closet and out the other side into the gym itself. 'Wow!

I never knew that was there,' Josie exclaimed, as she felt the familiar sights and smells of the gym take her over.

'I doubt you spent much time in the boys' change rooms,' laughed Brad, before picking up a loose basketball from the side of the court and starting to throw hoops. He moved with the grace and ease of a natural athlete, and Josie settled herself on the bleachers to watch him play, so reminiscent of 25 years before, when they were dating and the world was their oyster.

'You look good out there,' she called out playfully to Brad, who smiled and sank a ball with ease.

He then joined her on the bleachers and simply asked, 'So what's it like for you?'

Josie paused for a moment, thinking of what to say. She decided for complete honesty. What had she to lose?

'Busy. Challenging. And, to be completely honest, pretty stressful.' She looked him straight in the face. Josephine's honesty surprised Brad and made him feel uncomfortable. He didn't want to get too personal here—after all, he was only in town for this event, and then he was flying back to the States and his life.

He decided the safest course was to get her talking about the business she built—how she did it and what were her future plans.

Josie went through the beginnings of her business. How passionate she was and how she'd easily attracted clients who wanted to work with her. As her story went on, she realised how much she had learned about business over the years, and the industry she was in. She also felt pride that she could sit with Brad, who had achieved so much, and have something credible to say.

Brad listened carefully, asking questions here and there to clarify, and generally learning more about how she had built her company. He was impressed with her knowledge and confidence, and even more so by the fact that some of the CEOs she worked with were notoriously tough. She obviously could handle herself, and he got the sense that she took no prisoners—and that perhaps she was just as tough as the people she helped take to the next level in the business community.

'Your turn now,' said Josie, before asking Brad to tell her first-hand what he spent his time on. Brad outlined his latest projects, where his offices were around the globe and what he would be working on next. His list of achievements were well recorded in the press but what they didn't report, what Josie was most interested in, was just how much of Brad's blood, sweat and tears brought them to life.

As Josie was listening intently to Brad, they heard soft steps at the far end of the gym and towards the boys' change rooms. They also heard giggling and various shushing noises, and then watched as Karen and Russ, trailed by Jasper and Jayne, moved onto the court.

'Busted!' yelled Jasper as he spied the two of them on the bleachers. 'What's going on here?' he asked speculatively, noting how close the two of them were sitting.

'Nothing now that you're here,' Josie said coldly. Jasper had obviously had too many drinks and was definitely in party mode. She found it all so unattractive, and typical of the man who had never grown up past high school.

'We can go,' Karen chimed in quickly. She'd had no idea that Josie had come out here, and knew her friend would be disappointed she'd been interrupted.

'No need,' Brad quickly responded. He didn't want to get too deep with Josephine anyway. He was leaving in a couple of days and didn't want to give her the wrong idea.

The four settled on the bleachers near Brad and Josie and, true to form, Jasper pulled a large silver flask from his jacket pocket, took a swig and passed it onto Jayne, who took it hesitantly.

'Tequila,' Jasper mouthed, and Jayne raised it to her lips tentatively.

Jayne let out a gasp after quickly swallowing a mouthful and handed the flask to Brad. Surprisingly, Brad took a large mouthful and passed it onto Josie. Soon, the whole group had a turn and the flask found its way back to Jasper.

'Let's play truth or dare,' giggled Jayne, the effects of the tequila starting to kick in. 'I'll go first. Jasper—you pick. Truth or dare?'

'Dare, of course,' responded Jasper at once. The truth was something he was uncomfortable with at the best of times.

'I dare you to wear one of the uniforms in the change rooms,' Jayne giggled. 'Done!' was Jasper's reply as he trotted off to find some unlucky teenager's forgotten sports gear.

He soon came back in shorts that were more than a size too small, and a shirt that showed his midriff. He was glad he had not lost his athletic form, and while he still looked pretty stupid, it could have been a whole lot worse.

The group laughed as he sashayed around with a basketball, enjoying the attention of a crowd.

'You go next, Russ,' Jasper called.

'Truth,' said Russ quickly, not wanting to join Jasper in his dare antics. He hadn't kept his physique quite as trim and wasn't keen to show off his small gut.

'What's the worst thing about being married with kids?' Jasper yelled gleefully, pinning his friend in an impossible position with his wife sitting next to him.

Russ thought for a moment, myriad answers rushing through his mind. Deciding to answer honestly and not just through a funny, Russ responded.

'Not getting to enjoy it,' he said. Karen looked at him with worried eyes. What did Russ mean?

'I'm always working,' Russ explained, 'and I would much rather be hanging out with my beautiful wife and our kids. It's just impossibly busy.'

Karen was satisfied with the answer, and felt herself relax. Thank God this was what Russ considered the worst thing about being married to her.

Just then they heard the creak of the door again. Ben Jamieson appeared from the shadows and seemed surprised to find them all here. 'Sorry for crashing,' he said. 'I was just taking a trip down memory lane.'

# Chapter 11

# The truth comes out

'No problem,' said Jasper at once, and Ben laughed when he saw the uniform. 'Pull up a pew and take a shot of tequila.'

Ben sat down but said no to the tequila—it was one drink that even the smell of made him sick.

Jasper quickly filled him in on the truth or dare game, and nominated Josie for the next turn. She picked truth, and turned to Russ for the question.

'Who has been the greatest love of your life?' asked Russ. Karen kicked his ankle hard, not quite believing that Russ would ask such a question of Josie in front of Brad.

'Oh, that's easy,' said Josie. 'It's definitely myself,' she laughed, and so did everyone else. *Nicely handled*, thought Karen.

Everyone was relaxed and enjoying themselves, despite the differences in how they lived their lives. 'My turn,' squealed Jayne, and asked Brad to choose truth or dare.

'Dare.' He didn't want to expose himself by revealing any hard truths.

Jayne opened her purse and pulled out what looked like a hand-rolled cigarette. 'I dare you to take a drag on this.'

Jasper hooted with glee as he realised that Jayne had a joint. 'It's my ex-husband's,' she quickly explained. He had left it over 18 months ago, and on impulse Jayne had packed it into her bag for the reunion. She had not smoked in years, but thought Jasper might find it fun. Now she was handing it to billionaire Brad Malone like it was the most natural thing in the world.

'I will not inhale,' laughed Brad, imitating the famous Clinton line, but he took the joint and Jayne's lighter and went about the business.

Josie looked on in fascination. She had never known Brad to smoke anything in their time together, and was surprised at how easily he took up the challenge. Brad took a long draw and then handed the joint back to Jayne. She took a quick puff and handed it to Jasper. And so the circle all took turns at passing it around, until it was gone.

'Thank God we are staying at the hotel tonight,' Karen said very slowly, and heaved a sigh of relief. 'We all are!' whooped Jasper, to which Josephine rolled her eyes, knowing all too well she would be picking up that tab.

Ben had been sitting quietly, watching everyone in fascination. He hadn't touched the joint as it was handed around, and nobody had seemed to notice. He was definitely the outsider in this group. He was friendly with everyone, but hadn't hung around with them at school. This had been the 'in-crowd'—the popular kids—and even now seeing how they had turned out was like watching a science experiment.

'Okay, must be my turn to ask,' said Brad. 'Karen: truth or dare.' Karen knew she was never going to do an embarrassing dare, and quickly chose truth. Her heart was beating a little faster and it seemed surreal that Brad was focusing in on her.

'Biggest regret so far?' Karen stopped and thought for a while. She did not have any life regrets sitting on the surface of her mind.

'Well, if I had to pick something, I guess it would be that I stopped working,' she said truthfully. While she loved being a mother and a wife, she had watched Josie go from strength to strength in her career, and saw the freedom and choices that money and success gave her.

Russ looked surprised. 'Really?' he asked. He'd always assumed Karen enjoyed staying home and avoiding the pressure of work. In fact, at times he was jealous that home was all she had to worry about.

'It's not something I think about every day,' Karen said to him. The joint had made her more truthful and less willing to say things to please people around her. 'I just wish I had given myself more options — the kids will be all grown soon and I won't be able to do anything.' She started to look sad.

'Babe, you are the best mother I know — you will be kept busy with grandkids and being Sydney's version of Martha Stewart,' chimed up Josie, feeling bad for Karen and even a bit surprised. Karen hadn't told her this before, at least not for many years. Josie realised that most of the time their conversations were about her — her challenges and stresses, and what to do next. Karen spoke about the kids and Russ a lot, but rarely about herself.

Russ gave Karen an affectionate kiss on the cheek. 'We would be nothing without this incredible woman,' he said, making Karen look gratefully at him and smile.

Ben had seen this many times in marriages — where the woman had given up her career and working, and ended up with fewer options later in life. He wondered what financial position they were in.

Karen then looked directly and Jayne. 'Truth or dare?' She knew Jayne would most likely pick truth as she and Josie had done. Jayne, however, chimed up with dare.

'All right. I dare you to sit on Jasper's lap and give him a big old kiss,' laughed Karen. 'Yes!' whooped Jasper, and patted his lap eagerly. Jayne delicately stood up and perched herself on Jasper's lap. 'Pucker up, baby,' she playfully said and gave

Jasper a kiss that sent chills up his spine. In fact, the kiss was so intense that Karen called out to end it. 'Okay, okay, you took that dare and nailed it,' she said, as Jayne winked at her and sat back down in her seat.

Jayne then proceeded to tell everyone she hadn't kissed someone in well over two years, and tears started to well up in her eyes. By now everyone was feeling much closer, the barriers between them had dropped, and it seemed okay for Jasper to ask her about her divorce.

Jayne told them about her ex—his drinking and erratic mood swings, and how she'd found herself in a position she never thought she would be in. The worst part about it, though, wasn't even the stuff Jayne was telling them about—not the fear or the physical violence. The worst part was that deep down Jayne felt ashamed of herself. Ashamed she had been weak enough to let her husband physically abuse her. Ashamed her girls had heard their father screaming and swearing at their mother. She was educated and from stable parents. This kind of thing didn't happen to people like her.

This shame of her marriage failure, along with her deep disappointment and the feeling of disgust she had for herself, was so hidden, so unacknowledged. She felt weak for putting up with it for as long as she did, and furious with herself for picking that relationship to begin with. 'What a major cock-up,' she spat out bitterly. 'I'm such a weak woman.' The real anger in her voice made Karen look at her sharply.

'You can't blame yourself for someone using physical threats and violence toward you,' she said incredulously.

Josie agreed instantly. 'It's the lowest act—used by the most pathetic of men,' she assured Jayne.

'But I picked him,' Jayne said with tears in her eyes. 'It's my fault. I am so ashamed of what I've done, and what I put my girls through.'

Jasper looked at Jayne with real compassion and said, 'You have this great capacity for joy and love. I can see how any man would be attracted to that. I'm sure you were in love and so was he when you got together. Sometimes, life just gets harder over time, and it drives people to do things they never thought they would do. I am sure your ex is gutted deep down at losing you.'

Jayne looked surprised as she turned to Jasper. 'I'd never really thought of it from Nick's perspective,' she said. 'I bore the brunt of so much of his bad behaviour that I stopped wondering why a long time ago.'

Jasper knew he couldn't explain why Jayne's ex-husband had turned to drinking and becoming physical. But he did know a little at least about why people turned to drinking. It was a way to numb the voice in your head—the voice that said you weren't good enough, and were a joke, a disappointment to your family.

'Maybe he was ashamed of himself, Jayne. Maybe it was nothing to do with you.' His voice was full of emotion as Jayne put her head on his shoulder. Jasper was a good-hearted man. He never intended ill on anyone, and he was someone who deserved to allow themselves joy and love.

The group had sat and listened silently to the details of Jayne's marriage crumbling and Jasper's insight into Jayne's ex-husband. It was Ben who chimed up and asked about the divorce settlement.

'I've pretty much got nothing, except my gorgeous girls,' said Jayne. She explained her job in the law and how her parents had been a brilliant help to her. She also told them that Nick gave her $2000 a month for the two girls—but that the kids certainly cost more than a $1000 a month each when living in Sydney.

Ben had seen this many times too—women who had been left raising the kids, with a father who contributed some money but not enough to make life easy.

Jayne had been one of the most popular girls in school—athletic and sweet natured. It was a shame she'd married the wrong man.

Jasper felt awful for her, and respected how truthful she was being about her life. The words popped out before he could stop them. 'I live with my mother, in the bedroom I slept in while I was at high school.' The group looked at him, absorbing his confession.

Russ was surprised. While he knew exactly where Jasper lived, it was never discussed in a way that made it seem like Jasper needed to be there. Rather, Jasper talked about how much his mother needed him, and how he was only there out of love and duty for her.

'Yep, I'm admitting it. I am a 43-year-old loser. I have a job I hate, live with my mother—who I know does not need me there—and have no idea what's next for me in life.'

Jayne sat in silence. This was not the kind of man she was hoping to attract when she envisioned herself finding another love. But she knew admitting this to the group must have been hard for Jasper—even if it was aided somewhat by the tequila and smoking.

Russ looked at Jasper. 'Mate, why have you never said that to me? We've only been friends for 30 years.'

Jasper met Russ's eye and answered. 'Because you have the perfect life, Russ. Pretty hard to admit you're a loser to someone who has everything.'

Russ absorbed this information for a moment in silence. He then looked up. 'Do you know I don't sleep much anymore?' Karen held her breath as her husband continued. 'I lie in bed every night, thinking about a job that I can't stand, knowing I can't ever leave for something I really want to do. I have responsibilities. I have people who need me to make the money I do. My family is the most important thing in the world to me. But that means that what I want is not.'

'At least you have someone to dedicate your life to,' piped up Brad. The whole group turned to look at him. 'Money is no object to me. You all know that. And I'm sure you wonder what my life is like. Don't get me wrong, the work I do is incredibly important to me. It's the driving force in my life. But when I sit and look at Russ and Karen, and hear them talk about their kids, I realise that dedicating my life to work is a poor substitute for real live people who need me.'

Josie squeezed his hand and smiled sadly. 'I totally understand, Brad. I might not have achieved what you have, but I've built something substantial enough to realise that no matter what you have, it can't replace *who* you have. The only difference is your work inspires you, and actually changes the world for the better. I've built a business that makes powerful men more money and more power. And the minute I stop, it all crumbles around me.'

The group was silent as everyone's confessions sank in. Again, it was Ben who piped up. 'I suspect you're pretty leveraged, Josie. I reckon your cash flow is what's making you feel like everything will crumble if you stop.'

Josie looked at him in surprise. 'Well, I guess so, if you put it like that. I make a lot of money, but with all my overheads, I have to keep pumping it in to the black hole to make it all work.'

Ben had also seen this many times—successful people who got themselves into the trap of using one income to pay for several other assets as well as an expensive lifestyle. As long as the income kept coming in, things were fine. But if it stopped, the whole set up was like a wall of dominoes—one part knocking the next one down.

'Well, we seem like a pretty miserable lot!' Karen's laugh was brittle. 'I don't suppose my complaining about the continuous groundhog day of my life—cooking, cleaning, school runs and falling into bed exhausted—seems like much in comparison.' Josie reached out and squeezed her hand.

'Babe, I know what you do isn't easy. In fact, I'm in awe of how you make it all work. I don't think I could pull it off.'

Russ kissed his wife affectionately on the head. 'She is the absolute heart of our family. Without Karen, none of it would work.'

'Exactly!' cried Karen, with more passion than she'd intended. 'I'm the reason it all works. So if you feel trapped in what you do to make money, try being me! I don't make money. I don't do anything but be the family housekeeper and nanny. A job you hate is better than a job that pays nothing. And, at the end of it, I get left with no skills and no options—just waiting for grandkids to come so I can look after the next set of family members.'

Russ looked a bit shell shocked. He had never heard his wife talk like this before. Sure, he'd heard her complain about the washing, the cooking and the traffic on school runs. But he didn't know her unhappiness ran so deep. He felt ashamed that he was so worried about his burdens that he'd never really understood his wife's.

'How did it all get so hard?' asked Jayne. 'It was supposed to be better when we all grew up. We were supposed to do great things. We were supposed to be happy.'

They all looked at each other in a shared moment of realisation. No matter what people achieved, no matter how their life looked on Facebook, they all had problems. Each and every one of them had disappointments. Nobody felt their life was perfect, and all wanted to change at least one aspect of it.

Ben cleared his throat, and spoke in a voice that was both compassionate and wise. 'You know in my line of work, I see this every day. You may think I am exaggerating, but I'm not. As a financial planner, you would think I'm simply sorting out people's money. But most of the time, I am sorting out their lives.' He walked over to the chalk board where the basketball team kept scores.

'I'm going to share something with you all. It's not something I thought I'd be talking about at our 25-year reunion but it's something that I think can help you all. You can identify some of the things that may be holding you back. I like to call them areas of your life, and your finances, that you need to *unlearn*.' Ben looked again around the group. 'I know you guys. And I've met so many others just like you. You have to think that we're halfway through our lives now we're in our forties. Some of us may live longer than others, but we are all at a point where we have lived enough to know what brings us happiness, and also what's holding us back.'

The group looked on, intrigued.

# Chapter 12

# The unlearn pillars

He drew a large circle on the board. He wrote a heading that said 'The 5 unlearns' at the top of the circle. He then wrote five words around the circle. The first word was DESIRE.

'Have you ever wondered why we stopped building churches and starting building malls?' he asked. 'Our ode to stuff—consumerism—is one of the biggest traps of the western world. When our church is a shopping mall, what are we encouraged to do? We're encouraged to spend. And this spending comes at a heavy price—the freedom we don't have, because we're in debt. We're leveraged. And we have to keep working to pay for it all.'

'Jasper, pass that tequila around again,' Josie demanded, and everybody laughed. They all knew Josie was the most obvious candidate for unlearning desire.

'Josie, it's not just you who needs to really think about this. Who here has a big mortgage? Who here is trapped in a lifestyle they can barely afford? Who is miserable because of it?

Karen and Russ both shot their hands up. Looking at each other, they laughed. They felt like school kids again, both confessing they didn't know the answers.

'Pretty normal stuff, guys,' Ben continued. 'Most of Sydney would confess to the same thing. Yet we stay here, and pay up and stay miserable and change nothing.' Ben had many clients from the most affluent middle class suburbs, and he knew these suburbs often held the most miserable of people.

'Trying to look like you have it all but then peddling like crazy to keep it all going is a real misery trap. And the desire trap is just that — the trap that keeps us in a life that ultimately brings us misery.'

Karen caught Josie's eye. Unlearning desire made a lot of sense. Putting it into action, however, would take more work. 'Don't worry about solutions tonight,' said Ben reassuringly. 'Before you can solve problems, you need to acknowledge you have them. This gym, this night and these people are all part of this process.'

They all looked at each other in new light. None of them could have expected this was how the night would turn out when they first thought about going to the reunion. Yet they all felt a closeness like what they'd had at school. They doubted they would ever be confessing the reality of the lives without this reunion and this moment in time together.

Ben continued his writing in the circle. The next word he wrote was FOCUS.

'This is a big one — and it's the reason most people don't get what they want in the long term. Because what you focus on is what you get.' Ben underlined the word. 'Too many people focus on what's in front of them. The next holiday. The next job. The next party. The next crisis. Whatever it is, next is the order of the day. They forget the bigger picture of what they really want from their life overall.'

'I'm suspecting this one is aimed at me,' said Jasper a little glumly. Everyone had heard his confession that he was a life loser—still living with his mum, going from job to job. The truth was he'd never had a bigger vision for his life. Not since high school, anyway, when he dreamed of being a professional footballer. When that didn't happen, he didn't set himself any other big dreams—and so his focus remained small. Looking for the next party, or the next good time.

'This is a lot of people not just you, Jasper,' Ben explained. 'The funny thing about life is you usually get what you spend most of your time thinking about.'

'You know, that's my issue too,' said Jayne. 'I was so focused on getting married, getting a husband and having kids. When that fell apart, my focus ever since has been survival. Outside of finding someone else to love, I don't really have a bigger focus at all.'

Ben nodded encouragingly. 'There are no right and wrong answers when it comes to this stage of our lives—only realisations, and understanding what you want and what's not working for you anymore.' Ben knew from experience that, too often, people expected other people to bring them happiness.

'When your goal is a husband and kids, then there's a lot of expectation on that to be the biggest happiness bringer in your life. Without a focus on what *you* want for you, expecting other people to bring you happiness and fulfilment becomes impossibly hard.'

Karen looked down at her lap, feeling this resonated deeply. She adored her family and they all gave her intense moments of happiness, but she had lost sight of a big picture focus for herself. It was unrealistic to expect everyone else to bring her happiness, if she didn't have focus of her own.

Ben went back to the board again, this time writing the word TIME in another segment of the circle.

'This one is perhaps the hardest one of all to master,' said Ben. 'Because time can't be stopped. You can't go back and you can't get more.' Ben shook his head. 'So many people think they have all the time in the world. To get what they want. To have that great relationship. To plan for their retirement. But so many of us leave it too late.'

It was here Brad nodded. 'That one's mine'.

Everyone looked at him, amazed. If anyone had made good use of their time, it was Brad Malone. He was, after all, a billionaire. 'I've spent all my time working. No wife, no kids and no real relationship with my family,' Brad admitted quietly, suddenly embarrassed by how short-sighted he had been.

'Well, if money is the only measure of success, you are successful,' said Ben. 'But, if you value love, human connection and family, then, yep, you've used up your time on other things.'

Josie looked at Brad and smiled sadly. 'I totally understand what you mean,' she said.

'I'm pretty sure my mother ruined it for me,' Brad admitted, quickly giving the group a rundown on how much he'd always resented his overbearing mother for pushing him so hard.

'Brad, I know your mum,' Ben interjected. 'She belongs to our Rotary group. And, I have to say, she talks about you non-stop. She is incredibly proud of your achievements.'

'I bet she is,' said Brad bitterly. 'That's all she has ever been to me — someone pushing for me to achieve, to make her look good. I got over trying to please her a long time ago. Now I just try to forget, and avoid her.'

Ben nodded solemnly. 'You know, I would never normally share news this way, but it feels like the right moment to do it. Your mum has cancer. It's pretty advanced. She told our Rotary group a few months back to explain why she could no longer volunteer the way she used to.'

Brad sat in shock. This was not what he'd been expecting to hear. And he was unsure of how it made him feel. His mother dying? Why had she never told him? He then felt ashamed of himself. When could she? He never took her calls and rarely saw her. She got nothing from the son she had put so much of herself into. And now she was dying and he'd been told by someone else, by an almost stranger.

Brad sat in silence, unsure of what to say or how to feel. He was at least realising time was indeed something that he had not used wisely. This had turned into a most unusual night indeed.

'Brad, mate, I am so sorry to hear about your mum,' said Russ, breaking the silence. 'That's tough to hear, no matter what your relationship is like.' Brad nodded at Russ and stayed silent, not trusting his voice to speak. 'I guess time is also something Karen and I need to think about. While we have the house, we haven't planned our super at all, and I know Karen has been worried about that.'

Karen felt a surge at satisfaction at hearing this. So Russ did listen to her! And it seemed that secretly he shared the same fears as her.

'Tell me about it,' said Jayne. 'I know my super is nowhere near enough. I'm just counting on Mum and Dad to leave me their house.'

Jasper stayed quiet—admitting the obvious when it came to this one for him seemed pointless.

'I'm going to finish the circle,' said Ben, moving back to the board. The next word he wrote was BELIEF.

'This one is fascinating,' Ben explained, 'because it comes from both how you grew up and how much confidence you have in yourself. Look at Josie and Brad.' Both squirmed a little with the spotlight suddenly on them. 'Why do you think they have been so successful financially? Does anybody remember what they were like at high school? I know I do.'

'Josie was incredibly driven and determined,' said Karen. 'I always admired her for that.'

'So was Brad,' Josie piped up. 'That's what attracted me to him.'

She then seemed embarrassed that she had said that out loud, and looked to the ground.

'That's right,' said Ben. 'Do you think they both believed they would succeed? I know they did—in fact I wrote that in the school yearbook.' He turned back to the rest of the group. 'But let's look at everyone else's beliefs. Jasper—did you have any beliefs around money and your financial success?'

Jasper thought about it for a while. 'You know, I believed I was good at sport, and I wanted to have a good time. But I never believed I would make a lot of money. I guess Dad ground into me that you had to work really hard to make money—and that sounded pretty boring to me. So I avoided it.' Jasper looked like he was having a major realisation as he was saying this. He had never thought about his financial situation this way before. Who would have thought that those beliefs set up by his father could be a big reason he was in his current predicament, at his age?

'I bet we could all think of situations from our childhood where we developed beliefs that have limited us. You're certainly not the only one Jasper.'

Each of the group sat there thinking about how they grew up. It was a little shattering to realise that, while they were all grown up, they were still a product of their childhood.

'I guess I figured I would never be good at earning money,' Karen mused. 'My mother never worked and I always expected I would be like her. I always put all my belief in Russ. I guess that's been a lot of pressure for him.'

Russ looked at Karen and kissed the top of her head. 'Your belief in me has been the best thing that ever happened to me, babe,' he said sincerely. 'And I guess I work so hard to make money to prove in some way that my old man was wrong—that I could do more than a trade, be a better father than him. My mother deserved a lot more—at least I can do it for my wife.'

Ben looked pleased that the group really seemed to be embracing the principles of unlearning money and life.

'Now for the final part of the circle,' he said, writing the word ACTION on the board.

'Finally one I'm a fan of—getting some action!' laughed Jasper, while the girls rolled their eyes and both Russ and Brad hid a grin.

'Sorry, Jasper,' said Ben, 'but I don't mean that kind. I mean the kind of action that people take to get their lives in order—both financially, and from a life plan perspective. And, believe it or not, even if you have all the other unlearn pillars down pat, without this one, people will end up not having the life they really want.'

The whole group leaned forward at this. Ben was making sense—taking the right action was what it was all about. And, at their age, making wrong decisions had more than dire circumstances.

'This is what I spend my time doing as a financial planner. I help people identify what's really important to them, and then develop an action plan to help them get that,' Ben continued.

It was easy to see that Ben was very passionate about his work. 'Wow, you're a regular Dr Phil,' exclaimed Jayne admiringly, and with only a little teasing. 'But I doubt you could help someone like me. I don't have any left over money to make a plan with,' she finished truthfully.

'Don't be so sure, Jayne. I could probably help you build a plan very easily,' replied Ben with confidence. 'You have a decent income and some child support. You also have parents who will eventually leave you a financial legacy. If you plan correctly, and have up-front conversations with your parents sooner rather than later, I think you could have a great outcome for you and your girls—regardless of whether you remarry or not.' Jayne looked both hopeful and unsure—this was something she'd never imagined would be possible. 'Come and spend some time at my office, Jayne,' Ben said encouragingly. 'I would love to help you develop an action plan.'

Jayne smiled at Ben sheepishly. 'Will it be a freebie?' she laughed. She knew she could not afford financial advice. But, Ben had offered ...

'I am more than happy to help you,' Ben said directly. 'But I have to say, most people are wrong when they say they can't afford advice. We charge our clients a monthly retainer, rather than an up-front fee, and from the needs you say you have, you're probably looking at around $100 bucks.'

Jayne was genuinely surprised. 'I thought you had to pay thousands to get advice. That's why I never bothered before — I didn't think I had enough, or could afford it.'

Russ was impressed with Ben's charging model. Having worked in finance for years, he knew not everyone had their charges on retainer this way. It was a smart way to get people advice.

'Mate, I think Karen and I better come and see you too,' he said firmly. He had learned a lot tonight about his wife. It had both surprised him and made him feel ashamed that he hadn't given more time and thought to how his wife was really feeling. If he was honest, he'd taken advantage of the fact that she found expressing herself very hard. She just wanted to see him happy. But by not digging deeper and really tuning in with her, he'd lost the chance to really know her — as a best friend and a lifelong partner. He wanted more for their marriage than that.

'Well, I am going to figure out a way to earn some extra bucks at home,' said Karen resolutely. 'To pay Ben's retainer, and to put toward who we are next.' She turned to her husband. 'It's not just up to you, Russ.'

Karen felt the most confident she had in a long time. Normally she would never have put her hand up to try to earn money. She had always been worried that she wouldn't be able to handle both jobs — she was already so busy. But she was also smart, with a best friend who was a business guru, and kids who were good on the internet. She was going to come up with something.

Meanwhile, Ben stood by the scoreboard, grinning like a complete idiot.

'Check out the Cheshire cat,' laughed Josie, noticing his wide grin.

Ben was so excited because he knew, by building a plan together, Karen and Russ would go a long way toward being on the same path for life—not living two separate lives, and both of them resenting it. He also saw that they had experienced a breakthrough in their relationship—and he ticked a box in his head. He now knew for sure that his yearbook prediction that these two would grow old together and die happy like in *The Notebook* would come true. (Yes, his wife had made him watch the chick flick—and he'd ended up loving it.)

Ben knew to grow old together as true partners was perhaps the biggest goal of any marriage. Karen and Russ were going to make it.

# Chapter 13

# Yearbook predictions

A feeling of elation had definitely built among the group, and they hadn't felt so close in a long time. Laughter flowed easily, as did the usual teasing that went on with any group of Australian friends.

'Mate, I think you like wearing that sports uniform,' teased Russ to Jasper. 'If only you could go back in time.'

'Looks better on me than you,' retorted Jasper, running over to collect the ball and dribbling up and down the court again.

Ben was watching Jasper thoughtfully. 'Well, that would certainly match my yearbook prediction,' he said.

'What? That Jasper would be wearing teenagers' clothes at 43!' Russ burst out, laughing at his mate.

'Kind of,' Ben replied. Jasper looked at him indignantly. 'You can't have thought I was such a cock-up way back then, Ben?'

Ben leaned back and looked Jasper in the eye. 'Mate, I don't see you as a cock-up now. What I do see is someone who has always loved sport, who is naturally good at it, and who can make it fun for a whole bunch of other people. A team coach or sports teacher was where I predicted you would end up.'

Jasper looked surprised by this. He sat back down on the bleachers and thought about it for a minute. 'You know, I always wanted to be the sports star, not be the one coaching others. But, as you can all see, that hasn't happened.'

'So retrain!' piped up Jayne excitedly. 'You would be a great coach! 'Kids need fun and to be using sport as a way of blowing off steam. They'd have fun with you, but you'd also be someone they would trust.'

Jasper went slightly pink at this praise from Jayne. It had been a long time since anyone had said something positive about the impact he could have on the world. He had to admit, it felt good. But wasn't he too old to be thinking about going to university for at least three years? And how would he afford it? He barely scraped by as it was.

'I'll think about it,' he said, non-committally, but Ben wasn't going to let him get away that easily.

'Do more than that, Jasper. Come to my office and we can look at ways to use HECS to get the degree done. We can also have a think about what you could do part-time to make it all work.'

Ben was offering Jasper a lifeline. Something to aim for and define himself by — that wasn't centred on being a layabout for the next 30 years. 'It's too good an opportunity not to do it, Jasper,' interjected Jayne. 'I'm going to make sure you meet with Ben. Consider me your personal nagger.' She poked him in the ribs playfully.

'Jayne is right and, as usual, she makes a good argument,' piped up Ben, winking at her. 'That really is a reflection of the yearbook prediction I made for her.'

Jayne looked up quizzically at Ben. She could guarantee Ben had not predicted her life turning out the way it had. 'I actually thought you would be a great lawyer,' Ben explained.

'Oh, wow!' replied Jayne. 'You're like Nostradamus. When I did my law degree, that's exactly what I wanted to be.' Ben looked surprised. He hadn't realised Jayne had studied law.

'This is getting spooky,' giggled Karen. 'We didn't even know you'd made these predictions, and now they've turned out to be pretty spot-on in so many ways.'

Ben laughed with the group, denying that he had any magical powers that could help him see into the future. What he'd always had, even in high school, was a good understanding of people—what motivated them, and what talents they had and how they could use them. This understanding had very much helped him in his career as a financial planner, and meant he was able to help his clients dream about their potential again, no matter what age they were. It was his biggest gift.

'Tell us what's going to happen next, since you know so much,' said Josie, only half-joking. She'd been dreading the future for a while now, without even realising it. All this talk of what was meant to be and what change people could make was making her see that the way she was thinking had contributed to her stress and unhappiness.

'Well, that depends on what you do about tonight,' Ben responded. He knew that the only way any of them would see any improvement in their lives was to action change. All too often, people were given the information but chose not to act on it. They were too afraid of change, or they underestimated the time they had left to achieve what they wanted.

'We've all got a lot to think about,' said Brad seriously, as he reflected on his mother and the fact she was facing cancer. They nodded, all thinking about everything that had been revealed that night. It was as if they had all come together at exactly the right time, to each learn something about themselves. And, more importantly, what they needed to *unlearn*—both about money and about life.

'Well, we may as well finish this tequila,' piped up Jasper, as he handed around the flask again. It was now well after 2 am and Ben stood up to leave. 'My wife will think I've been kidnapped!' he said, before heading to the exit. The group clapped as he walked away, and Jayne's wolf-whistle echoed around the gym.

It was the first time Ben had ever been cheered at the gym and he smiled as he left the boys' change rooms. That was something he'd never predicted in his yearbook.

The others continued to drink and talk, catching up on the years and reflecting on the future. Their masks had dropped and they were as completely themselves as they had been in high school. It felt good to feel young again. It felt good to feel hopeful, and to be together.

As they noticed the sun coming up from the windows, they started to stir. 'Come on,' called Jasper, 'the Breakfast Club needs to eat!'

Karen laughed. Of all the movies from the '80s, *The Breakfast Club* was her favourite. 'Screws fall out all the time,' she quoted. 'The world's an imperfect place.'

*It sure is*, thought Josie as Karen smiled, scrolling through her iPhone to find the soundtrack to the movie. She hit play and 'Don't you (forget about me)' rang out through the gym as they all started to leave. Jasper walked ahead and punched the air, just like Judd Nelson in the classic film. 'I have goose bumps,' squealed Jayne. 'We are living that movie.'

'And we're 43 years old,' laughed Josie, linking arms with Karen.

They pushed the door open and walked into the light. They were headed to breakfast and then to their future—and, suddenly, it seemed bright again.

# Chapter 14

# The morning after

Breakfast had never tasted so good. They all went to Josie's suite at the hotel, and lay around eating room service. Jasper had had the brilliant idea to order robes for everyone via housekeeping. While Josie rolled her eyes when he picked up the phone, she had to admit it was cool to all be lounging while picking at the bacon, eggs, fruit, muffins, croissants and various other items she and Karen had ordered.

They all felt so comfortable with each other. Brad and Josie were sitting on the bed leaning against the headboard, with Karen and Russ at the bottom of the bed. Jayne and Jasper were on the couch with their feet on the coffee table, and the room looked like a university common room.

'God, I am so glad my parents have the kids,' giggled Jayne as she sipped on her coffee and nursed what was turning out to be a slight hangover.

'Definitely not in the mood for kids,' agreed Karen, although she had to admit her thoughts had turned to them this morning, wondering how they were all getting along.

'We will all be back to normal soon enough,' Russ reminded them. At this, they all went silent, thinking about what lay ahead of them and what had gone before.

'We've all got some big challenges ahead,' said Josie as she gently squeezed Brad's hand. Rather than take his hand away, Brad left it there. Her hand felt good in his and, somehow, she gave him courage to face what was ahead.

Jasper watched them both with interest. He realised that Josie looked a lot happier than she normally did, and it suited her. He knew she had disapproved of him for the longest time and, in his heart of hearts, he knew he deserved it. He hoped that last night would be a turning point for him, and he could win back the respect of people who had lost faith in him over the years. He felt more determined than he had in a very long time.

He wondered if Jayne had lost interest in him, now that she knew the truth about his financial situation. He wouldn't blame her if she had. She had a lot to contend with. He playfully nudged her foot, and offered her a bite of his muffin. She took a huge playful bite, leaving him to pull away in mock horror. 'What happened to a delicate nibble?' he protested.

'Jasper, you need to know this about me. I don't just take a taste. The big bite is how I roll.'

Jasper knew at once that Jayne was talking about more than breakfast. She was saying she was all in, or nothing at all. He found himself feeling both nervous and excited at the thought. She was the most positive thing that had happened to him in a long time.

Russ watched Jasper and Jayne together. To his surprise, Jasper was acting like someone who was interested in more than just a good time. Russ thought about all the girls he'd seen with his mate over the years. Jasper had never seemed serious about any of them. This was something different and, he had to say, he approved. It was about time that Jasper let someone see another side of him. Russ knew him well enough to know he was a kind-hearted and decent bloke deep down. That's why they'd stayed best friends for so long. It was good that the rest of the group was getting to see this side of Jasper.

Karen wiggled her toes and admired her pedicure. 'Josie, I sure could get used to this life,' she laughed, snuggling into her fluffy hotel robe. 'Let's do it every year!' Josie piped up. She too was enjoying herself more than she had in years, and she just didn't want it to end.

'Great idea,' said Brad, and squeezed her hand. Suddenly a trip to Sydney every year made perfect sense. 'In fact, I'll be here at least twice a year, so next time let's stay on my boat,' he suggested.

'Only if we all get our own rooms,' joked Jasper in mock outrage.

'That shouldn't be a problem — it has seven double bedrooms with ensuites,' replied Brad and Jasper whistled.

'Mate, what's it like to be that rich?' he asked. The way he asked was both respectful and curious and, for the first time in a long time, Brad felt comfortable talking about it.

'It's a responsibility,' said Brad. He thought for a moment before he continued. 'So many people rely on me to get things right. From the house staff to the people I employ around the world, my actions have repercussions for so many more than just me.'

'Wow! I had never thought of your life that way,' Russ piped up. 'That's the way I feel about my life and my family — but you literally have that on a global scale.'

'In a lot of ways, Russ, what you have is more meaningful — because you can see your family thrive and return your love. In business, there's no love. Plenty of ambition, drive, even passion, but no love.'

'I get it,' nodded Josie. 'The more I earn, the deeper I go — into responsibility and the fact that you can never get away from it. It becomes part of your DNA and your life — people see you from the outside and think you have it all but, in actual fact, you don't have time to find out who you really are. You're so busy keeping up the momentum. The momentum can swallow you whole—but, without it, you can't achieve.'

Brad knew exactly what Karen was talking about. He had incredible discipline and energy, but he had also found the momentum to be an all-engulfing beast—without it, however, things started to fall apart. While you relied on other people to run a business of scale, you knew without you at the mast, the ship was going to lose the wind and slow down—or, worse still, take the wrong path.

'All right, enough! You guys are so serious,' teased Jayne. 'What's it like to be able to buy whatever you want?'

Brad smiled. 'Fair point,' he conceded. 'By now, I take it for granted. And, to be honest, I'm not really a massive spender on things. But I do remember when I got my first private plane. That was a buzz.'

Karen clapped her hands and laughed. 'That's so celebrity! How awesome.'

Josie smiled at her friend's enthusiasm. She had to admit a private plane was pretty damn cool. She'd known people who had their own, but was nowhere near that level herself. That was one of the differences between millionaire and billionaire.

'All this talk of money is making me hungry again,' piped up Jasper. 'We need more bacon.'

Josie lobbed the hotel phone at his head, which he deftly caught and pressed 9. *This room service gig is the best*, he thought.

So the six of them continued to drink coffee, eat bacon and eggs, and catch up on the past 25 years. There were no pretences, and no holding back. They were themselves.

At about 10 am housekeeping knocked at the door. 'Come back later,' called out Josie, but she knew her late checkout would end at midday, and that they were going to have to pack up.

'I hate to call it people, but we need to make a move.' Everyone groaned. They all knew it was time to go back to their lives, but the thought of again becoming who they were yesterday was heavy.

They all slowly got up, took off their robes and straightened their evening wear. It was time to be grown-ups again. Jayne and Jasper were the first to go. They caught a cab together, because their places were close to each other. They held hands in the back of the cab and Jayne rested her head on Jasper's shoulder.

'What a fantastic night,' she mumbled, half-asleep. Jasper smiled and smoothed her hair with his hand affectionately. 'It sure was,' he whispered.

Russ and Karen left next, after Karen gave Josie a big hug. 'I'll call you tonight,' she promised as she and Russ left to go back to the kids. Brad stood at the door with Josie and shook Russ's hand. 'Keep in touch, mate,' he said, and Russ could tell by the sound of his voice that he meant it.

When it was just Josie and Brad left in the room, the vibe immediately shifted. Suddenly Josie wondered whether her hair was looking like she'd been dragged through a bush backwards. Brad, on the other hand, wondered how she could look so good after not sleeping all night.

He delicately rubbed a finger across her jawline, and murmured, 'Still so beautiful,' under his breath.

Josie put her hands on his chest and looked into his eyes. The moment was charged with intimacy and longing, and it seemed like the most natural thing in the world for Brad to bend down to kiss her lips. His kiss was tender and slow, and Josie moved closer into his arms. It felt both familiar and exciting.

After a moment, Brad pulled away slowly. Josie looked up at him with uncertain eyes. 'Let's just take this slow,' he said. He realised that the last time he'd pulled away from Josie they'd not seen each other for 25 years. He had no intention of losing her that way again, but he also knew that they lived on opposite ends of the world, both with loads of responsibility.

Josie nodded and smiled. She knew what he meant. If she threw herself in now, she would have her heart broken all over again. It was a promising start, but it was only the beginning. And she knew after the night they'd had, lots was about to change.

'I'll see you very soon,' Brad said gently, as he moved toward the door. Josie smiled and brushed her hair from her eyes, exactly the way she had done when she was seventeen years old. Brad took a sharp breath—leaving her was harder than he'd expected. He turned back to her and kissed her again—harder this time, more urgent and demanding. Josie responded and they both felt their breaths becoming deeper.

Josie pulled away this time. She knew if she didn't, housekeeping was going to find them in a compromising position.

'Text me your cell phone number,' said Brad, scribbling his number on the hotel notepad. He made up his mind then and there that he was not going to lose this woman again. 'I will,' said Josie, and blew him a kiss as he walked to the door.

The reunion had made them both realise one thing—deep down, they were not that much different from when they were in high school. Life had gotten very serious, and so had they, but it didn't have to remain that way.

After Brad left, Josie had a shower. She let the warm spray run down her face and, for the first time in a long time, looked forward to the future.

# Chapter 15

# 'The Breakfast Club' on paper

When Karen and Russ got home, they were relieved to see the house and the kids in one piece. Sure, there were dishes in the sink, the dishwasher hadn't been loaded and the table had crumbs all over it, but that was a small price to pay for the night off they'd had.

Karen's mind was ticking over. She'd been serious when she'd told Russ she was determined to contribute financially to their lives. She had to come up with an idea to make money.

Russ, on the other hand, was still thinking back about the events of the night. How life was not easier even when you had billions like Brad, and how Jasper had admitted so much about his own situation that not even Russ knew about. Things were not as they'd appeared yesterday.

They both were exhausted and needed some sleep. In a snap decision, Karen told the kids they didn't have to do their sports today. The announcement produced a mixed reaction, and Taz ran straight to the PlayStation. Karen was too tired to tell him to get off, and left the kids to their own devices as she and Russ went for a few hours' sleep.

As they both drifted off to sleep in their usual spoon position, Karen felt the familiar arm of Russ around her waist and smiled softly as her world faded to black.

*** 

On the other side of the city, Ben was busy juggling sports commitments with his wife. He'd drawn the short straw and was taking his son to cricket—which, at six hours, was a big commitment of time when he was so tired. But it did give him time to think, and he grabbed his trusty leather notebook on the way out the door. He had a few ideas on strategy for some of the guys from school and he wanted to shape his thoughts.

His thoughts first went to Karen and Russ. He really felt they'd had a breakthrough last night, communicating the way they had. And he knew the scenario all too well. Kids in private school, big mortgage, busy lives. They needed a circuit breaker.

He'd heard Karen say her parents lived on the coast, and this got him wondering. He knew they had two kids in high school and one in primary. He wondered just what year the kids were in, and jotted down the question in his notebook after settling his fold-up chair under a tree in the shade and pulling on his sunglasses. He was glad he hadn't drunk the tequila—he was tired as it was, and a hangover would have made it worse.

He wondered about what debt they had outside their mortgage. He got the feeling they must have some credit card debt from what Karen had said, and he made a note to find out how much.

He'd also need a valuation on their home. He knew they lived in an upwardly mobile suburb and had renovated. Their home was going to be a big part of any strategy for those two.

After thinking about Karen and Russ for a while longer, and writing down questions relating to aspects like super and insurance, his mind moved to Jayne.

Hers was a tough situation to be in. While it sounded like her ex did pay some child support for the twins, living in Sydney was expensive and the girls were still young—things tended to get more expensive the older kids got. He jotted down a few new notes, and remembered Jayne said her parents lived close to her in the family home where Jayne grew up. He speculated on the value of that house, and wrote a few notes on that. He also wrote down some questions about the rent amount, super contributions, working hours and child care.

He believed Jayne could be helped. He hoped she had the courage to ask him but, even if she didn't, she was one person he knew needed great advice. He checked his phone to make sure he'd gotten her number last night. He had, and he nodded in satisfaction. Jayne was getting a call from him next week.

He wondered what had happened with her and Jasper. Things certainly looked cosy last night, but he didn't think they'd been seeing each other for long outside of the reunion. They looked infatuated with each other, but it appeared that was all it was for the moment. He reflected on what Jasper had revealed about himself. This was the guy everyone had loved in high school. He was the classic jock who was good at most sports—which, like in most Australian high schools, had turned him into a god. While Ben had never been terrible, he had never excelled at any sport enough to get noticed, and he remembered wondering what it would be like if he were good.

But Jasper was a teenager no longer, and it appeared he'd lost much of his identity when he failed to make a career out of sport. Ben wondered about Jasper's mother and her financial situation. He knew his dad had died and he was living in his mother's house. Did she have money saved outside of the house? Did she have a retirement plan for what was coming next?

He scribbled some more notes, and then turned his mind to university. If Jasper went full-time to uni to study, he could finish the degree in three years. If he went part-time to do teaching, he would finish in five. At 43 years old, he needed to get moving either way, and Ben scribbled down some ideas on items like living expenses, HECS debt and property value.

He knew Brad wasn't going to need financial advice, but he certainly could check in with him regarding his mum. The news seemed to have rattled him quite a bit, and Ben knew Brad only had limited time to repair his relationship with his mother. Her cancer was quite aggressive apparently, and with Brad living in the United States, it didn't seem possible that he would be able to spend much time with her. Ben decided to check in with Margaret Malone and see how she was doing. He also felt he should give her the heads-up that he'd revealed her illness to her son. While normally he would never dream of doing such a thing, he'd felt if he didn't Brad would miss a valuable opportunity to make things right with someone who had obviously been instrumental in making him who he was today.

That left Josie for Ben to think about. Of all of them, Josie seemed the most burdened. He suspected that she was in a lot of debt — or what those in the business world called 'leverage'.

Debt was one of those things that tended to have a crushing effect on the soul, Ben believed. So many of his clients had become overcome with debt, and it had destroyed their lives. The need to keep the cash rolling in to pay for all the components of life was obviously weighing heavily on Josie. He quickly grabbed his phone and Googled her business and found her website. It was incredibly impressive, and Ben whistled quietly to himself.

This was clearly someone who got things done. She was self-made and ambitious, but it seemed her achievements were no longer giving her as much joy as they once did. Ben started to make notes on things to talk to Josie about — aspects like her overheads for her business, and how much her people costs were versus fixed costs. He wondered whether she owned her property. He remembered she'd mentioned a place in the Hunter she owned, and he wondered how many more properties she had. He also wondered about her succession plan for her company. The business looked very much tied to her as the principal, and he wondered if she had a strategy at all for how she was going to exit.

So many times he had seen clients build successful businesses, only to realise it was so tied to them that it was worth nothing to sell. Good succession planning took time and strategy. It was at least a five-year process in Ben's mind, and Josie would be almost 50 in five years. Had she thought about what next? He made a note to ask.

Last night had certainly been an interesting night. Ben hadn't expected to get in so deep with people at the reunion — particularly the set of people who, at high school, had been the cool kids. He had to admit, however, he'd really enjoyed teaching them about the five principles of unlearning money and life. They were all intelligent adults, but he could tell what he'd said had made an impact. He also had a feeling they would act on the information and make their lives better. He was determined to help them — not because he needed new clients (he could have shut the doors of his thriving practice if he wished) but because he genuinely wanted to help. He knew that, with some good advice and a solid plan, all of them could reinvent the parts of their lives that were bringing them down and causing them stress.

Just then he heard a shout from the cricket pitch. His son had been caught out while batting. 'Bad luck, mate,' he shouted, and one of the other dads walked over to have a chat. Ben knew it was time to stop thinking about work and focus on the game. He put away his phone and closed his leather notebook before standing up to shake the hand of another parent giving up their Saturday for kids sport. He had plenty of time to talk with each member of the Breakfast Club. Now, though, it was time to focus on his kids.

# Chapter 16

# Action

Karen woke up with a start, scrambling for the clock on her bedside table and realising it said it was 3 pm. 'Oh my God!' she cried, and elbowed Russ in the ribs. Russ opened one eye sleepily and grunted. 'Wake up, babe.' She swung her legs over the side of the bed. God knows what the kids were up to — although she had a sneaking suspicion that Taz would still be on the PlayStation.

Sure enough, he was — surrounded by wrappers, water bottles and a half-empty packet of biscuits. Taz was in the zone. The other two were in their bedrooms, headphones on, looking at their laptops.

Karen felt both relieved that everyone was okay and annoyed that technology was the main focus of their kids' lives when they were unsupervised. It was a constant struggle to get them off screens and into the real world — and one her parents never had to deal with. She wondered what this would mean for them as grown-ups — particularly Taz, who had been exposed to technology and screens practically from birth.

She had noticed kids at his school who seemed to have the 'faraway stare' she knew to be an overdose of screens. It was hard work getting kids to do other things when home, she knew that all too well. She also knew that mums who worked would struggle even more with keeping their kids busy and active. She worried to herself that her ambitions to make money would come at the expense of her kids.

'Well, other women do it, so I can too,' she said to herself determinedly. She was not going to let her fears and worry about the kids stop what she proclaimed to Russ and their friends last night. It was time for her to challenge herself. Now, what could she do?

Karen thought about all the things she did as a mum. Before kids, she had been an executive assistant. She'd enjoyed it, because she loved ticking off lists and being organised. She also loved getting things at the right price—and this was something she had become very good at as a mum. She found the best prices on everything from second-hand uniforms to school books—in fact, most of her friends asked for her advice on these things every year when school started.

This really got her thinking. Could she make a business from people wanting her advice on those sorts of things? She always heard Bella talking about online communities, and how she loved watching videos like the online tutorials her favourite make-up artists would give. Those people had hundreds of thousands of followers. They were online celebrities.

Could she make a community based around mums who wanted advice and tips? Ideas on the best prices, easiest ways to cook, getting ready for school, and the million other things she had developed skills at by being a mother of three?

She had to wonder. If people followed her, could she make money? She was uncertain on that part, but she knew someone who would be able to give her great advice. Josie would certainly assess it and tell her quickly whether the idea could make money or not.

She went to Nate's door and, after a quick knock, sat on the bed beside him as he reluctantly pulled the headphones from his head. 'What's up, Mum?' He had that resigned tone to his voice, indicating he just knew she was going to ask him to do a chore.

'Could you build me a website?' Karen asked. Nate's eyes widened and his mouth hung open. He'd been expecting her to tell him to clean his room, or make a start on homework. Not to build a website.

'What kind of website?' he asked.

Karen explained her idea of providing tips and advice for mums who were learning the ropes when their kids went to school. 'Cool idea, Mum,' said Nate enthusiastically, explaining that creating a website in WordPress should be pretty easy, and that he could even use a plug-in like Shopify so she could sell things like books and school year planners.

'Wow, Nate, that sounds amazing!' said Karen, looking in wonder at her son, and wondering how she ever got so lucky to have a kid like him.

Bella wandered past the room at this point in the conversation. She noticed the animated look on her mother's face and stuck her head in to figure out what was going on.

'Mum's going to be an online business owner,' said Nate, wrapping his arm around his mother's shoulders and giving her a hug.

'What?' squealed Bella, insisting immediately that Karen and Nate tell her all the details.

'Mum, you're going to need cool images to really sell this. You know, photography of you doing things that you're explaining, and a great pic of you that highlights who you are and what your mission is.'

'I guess you're right,' said Karen, amazed that both her children knew so much about the online world. 'I'll be your stylist and online creative,' said Bella excitedly, before twisting her hair on one side like she did whenever she was thinking deeply.

'I don't want this to take away from your school work,' said Karen, suddenly going back into 'Mum mode'. While it appeared her children would be more than helpful at implementing the idea, she always put them first and didn't want to put any more strain on their lives.

'Mum, we would love to help you,' said Nate, and Bella clapped her hands delightedly.

'We're so proud of you, Mumsy! It's a brilliant idea!'

Karen beamed. She hadn't felt this excited about something for herself for a very long time. She couldn't wait to tell Josie all about it. She gave both her offspring a kiss on the forehead, and went off to call her. As she walked away, they both started looking at website templates and photo styles. This was definitely the upside of the technology generation. And she could only imagine how good it would be for the kids if it worked, and the first-hand lessons they would gain about online business. This really was a brilliant idea.

Karen settled down on her comfy chair in her bedroom and texted Josie. Within seconds her phone rang. Josie had just woken up, and was dying to debrief with her best friend.

'OMG, what a night!' she exclaimed, as both of them began going over the detail of the night and its revelations. 'What happened after we left?' asked Karen, wondering just how far her friend had gone with Brad. She wouldn't blame her if it was all the way. She had been incredibly impressed with Brad — his authentic conversation and all around 'good guy' behaviour had Karen convinced that Josie may well end up with him.

'Nothing much,' said Josie, before dropping that they'd kissed passionately. Karen squealed with delight, and wanted to know how Josie felt.

'To be honest, I'm not sure,' replied Josie. This was not what Karen had expected.

Josie went on to explain that while she was still incredibly attracted to Brad, she also knew that they lived an ocean apart, and that both their jobs meant it would be impossible to spend any meaningful time together.

'That doesn't have to be the case forever,' said Karen, a tad disappointed that her friend was not trying harder to pursue love. 'Don't give up on him, Josie. I saw the way he looked at you. I know he still loves you.'

The phone went silent as Josie started to get tears in her eyes. This was way more complicated than she'd expected. 'I'm going to make an appointment to see Ben,' she said finally. 'The business and everything has me pretty worn out. I need to see if I can change my world a bit.'

Karen thought this was an excellent idea. She'd been thinking that she and Russ needed to see Ben too. He had raised so many good points last night that it made sense to involve him in the next stage.

It was then that she filled Josie in on her idea for an advice community for mums. When she finished explaining, Josie immediately expressed her approval. 'I love it!' she enthused. She went on to advise the business would be perfect to promote on Facebook. 'Build it and they will come,' she reminded Karen, and promised to introduce her to an online marketing guru she knew that owed her a favour.

Karen knew in her heart that if Josie thought it was a good idea, it was a winner. She trusted her friend's business instincts implicitly. They chatted for a little longer, and both agreed to make appointments with Ben and keep taking action to make their lives even better. They were both determined to reinvent their lives for the next chapter and, while they knew it couldn't happen in a day, they also knew the longer they waited the longer it would take. It was weird how one night together could have such a big impact, but they both agreed it had been a game changer—for more reasons than one.

Josie told Karen she was so impressed with Russ, and the way he had spoken about Karen and her contribution to the family. 'He's a damn good husband, Karen,' she said admiringly, and Karen agreed. Having Russ on her side, and really understanding how she was feeling, was perhaps the biggest win of the night.

She decided then and there to make sure Russ knew how much it meant to her.

They both chatted for a bit longer before hanging up. Josie Googled Ben's business and shot off an email to make an appointment for the following week. At the same time, Karen texted Ben to organise a time to go with Russ. Ben had been a big catalyst for all of them last night, and she knew he could help more.

Russ was in the kitchen, making them both a coffee. His hair was sticking straight up at the back and he looked like a teenager again. Karen went up behind him and gave him a big hug.

He turned around and put his arms around her to hug her back. He looked at Karen with a cheeky grin and asked if she was going to be the next Mark Zuckerberg.

'What?' she replied realising that the kids must have told Russ about her website idea. Suddenly she got worried. What if Russ thought it was a stupid idea? What if he was worried about the impact on the kids?

'Babe, it's a brilliant idea, and I know you can make it successful. You know so much about running a family—I am learning off you constantly. If you can't make it work, then nobody could.'

Karen felt like she was floating on air. She couldn't believe it. Her husband was supporting her, her best friend was helping her and her kids were her business partners. This was a dream come true—and to think only yesterday it wasn't even on the table.

She hugged her husband as hard as she could, until she could hear him laugh. 'Are you trying to give me a chiropractic session?' he asked as he extricated himself from her grip. Karen was so excited she didn't mind the teasing, and told him to watch out for what else she might be squeezing on her husband.

Russ raised an eyebrow but looked interested. It had been quite a while since Karen had made threats of this nature. His mind turned to last night, and everything they had talked about with Ben.

'I think we should make an appointment to see Ben,' he said. Karen grinned to hear her husband also thought Ben could add value to their future. She decided not to add that she had already sent a text asking for an appointment and, instead, smiled sweetly before replying, 'I think so too. I'll get us a time to see him.'

Russ was happy that Karen agreed. He had been more than surprised at her outburst last night and at how little she felt her contribution mattered. He'd realised he needed to support any ambitions his wife had — and he knew these could only be in the best interests of their entire family anyway. If Karen was happy, and if she did manage to earn an additional income, it would change their family dynamic considerably. It would also take some of the pressure off him to earn. He certainly wasn't hoping to relieve himself of all responsibility, but he would love to share the load. He would also like to spend more time with the kids. They were growing up fast, and Nate and Bella would be off to university in a few years. He didn't want to miss having more experiences with all three of them before it was too late.

He considered his idea to move jobs. While he was tired of where he was, he realised a move into something like funds management would be even more of a time commitment. The money would be good, but he wouldn't get to see the kids as much as he would like.

This was something he hadn't considered before when he was thinking of moving. He now knew he had to sit on the thought for a while before he made any moves. He hoped a professional conversation with Ben would also provide more clarity.

He handed Karen her coffee and wandered out onto the back porch to ponder. He realised with some annoyance that the lawn needed mowing, but right now was not the time for him to be doing chores. He had a slight headache, and wanted to think.

Karen followed him out and sat beside him on their outdoor couch, her head on his shoulder. Normally she would tell him straightaway that the lawn needed doing, not to mention the edges. But today she just sat and enjoyed the moment with her husband. After all, the lawn would wait.

# Chapter 17

# New beginnings

Jasper woke up feeling something he had not felt in a very long time—happy. He'd had a brilliant night with his friends and, for the first time in a long time, he felt he had something more to look forward to than just the next good time.

He also reflected on his new-found friendship with Jayne. They had caught a cab back to their respective homes together and, as Jayne got out, they had shared a small but intimate kiss.

He'd winked at her as she left the cab and said he would call her today. Now he reached over to pick up his phone and sent her an emoji blowing a kiss. Within seconds he got one back. He never would have guessed how much happiness an emoji could bring a 43-year-old man.

He swang his legs out of the bed and stood up, stretching. He didn't have a hangover—years of drinking had conditioned him to pull up fine. He did, however, have a serious need for coffee. He wandered to the kitchen and found his mother sitting at the kitchen table reading a magazine. She hadn't yet seen he was there and, as he looked at her sitting there alone for a moment, he realised his mother looked old. He'd never really thought about it before, but the sun was highlighting her silvery grey hair and her skin looked translucent—fine and papery. *She must be 75*, he mused to himself, thinking he would definitely have to do something special for her birthday coming up in November.

She looked up and saw him standing there. He went over and gave her a kiss on the cheek. Her face transformed as she glowed with happiness. 'What was that for?' she asked.

'Just because you are an excellent mum,' he answered back, and went to make them both a coffee. His mother watched him, her eyes narrowing.

'This doesn't have anything to do with Jayne, does it?' she asked suspiciously. She'd warned Jasper about that, and didn't want him taking advantage of the girl. She knew her parents after all, and certainly didn't need to avoid them because of another mistake her son had made.

Jasper looked her in the eye as he handed her a coffee. 'Sort of, Mum, but it's more than that.' And for the first time in many years, Jasper sat with his mother and talked about his life, and about how unhappy he was with how he had ended up. At this, his mother started to look slightly offended—after all, he had ended up living with her.

'Don't make it about you, Mum,' Jasper said, but with kindness in his voice. 'You know it's not ideal for a 43-year-old man to be living with his mother, and have no savings behind him.'

Jasper's mum could hardly argue with that. In fact, more than anything she felt relief that her son was talking like this. Could it be that he was finally growing up?

She knew that Jasper's dad had done him no favours with the way he talked about the responsibility of work and how tough it was. How hard it was to make money. He had been an immigrant from Yorkshire, and, for him, life had been hard. He had worked up to 18 hours a day to provide for their family and buy this house. But, in doing that, he'd missed vital time with their son and given their son the impression that life was tough and work was, in Jasper's take on it all, to be avoided if you didn't want to end up like him.

She patted her son's hand and made soothing noises. While all grown up, he was her only baby and she loved him deeply. Perhaps that love had allowed him to not have to grow up — after all, she would always be there to look after him. He smiled at his mother and blurted out, 'I'm thinking of going back to school.'

His mother looked surprised, to say the least. This was not what she'd expected. 'Tell me more,' she said with genuine interest.

Jasper explained how everyone had said last night how great he was at making sports fun. He loved being around teenagers, and missed the thrill of competitive sport at school. He thought he would make a good coach, or a PE teacher for high school. He acknowledged it wouldn't pay a lot, but it would be a job he could enjoy, and could do for the next 20 years.

His mother was elated. It was a fantastic idea, and with Jasper always having been so good at sport, it made perfect sense. She marvelled at how one school reunion could bring about so much change in her adult son. For her, it was bordering on a miracle.

Jasper then went on to talk about all the things Ben had said. How he could study part-time or full-time, and that they could come up with a practical plan to make it happen. 'He sounds like a pretty smart man,' his mother told him. 'Perhaps we should go and see him together. I have never had financial advice and it's about time I plan for my future too.'

Jasper looked surprised. He'd thought she intended to stay in the house and be wheeled out like his father.

'Okay, Mum, it's a date,' he said with enthusiasm as he picked up his phone to make a suitable time for them to visit Ben. He never could have imagined them going to see a financial planner together. Then again, he never could have imagined him going to university. Life sure did throw you curve balls.

\*\*\*

Meanwhile, Jayne was wrangling the pigtails of two eight-year-olds getting ready for ballet. No matter how many times she did their hair, they always ended up with wispy bits on the side. She knew the ballet teacher looked disapprovingly at things like that, and didn't want the girls to get in trouble.

Nan and Pop had let them stay up until 10 pm last night, and they were both a little grumpy. While Jayne was grateful that her parents had once again minded the girls, she did wish they would stick her to rule of 8.30 bed time. Late nights always made the girls harder to handle the next day.

She also knew she had a mountain of work to get through that night before the new week started again on Monday. She started to feel stressed — a very familiar feeling indeed. It was then that she received Jasper's emoji, and her mood immediately brightened.

It had been a brilliant night, one that she would remember for a very long time. It had felt good to confess everything she felt about the way her life turned out — and to think that she had the opportunity to change her situation was bordering on unbelievable.

But Ben had seemed confident she could. She decided then and there that she would make a formal appointment with Ben and tap into his expertise. She picked up the phone and called her parents.

'Mum, I'm thinking of seeing a financial planner friend of mine next week,' she said when her mother picked up the phone. 'Will you have the girls?'

Her mother was silent on the other end of the line, and then clicked to speaker phone so her father could hear as well. She could hear her getting her dad up to speed.

'They'll probably just try to sell you something,' she heard her father say. Jayne clicked her tongue in disappointment. Her dad was very fixed in his views, and she'd often heard him complaining about untrustworthy planners while reading the finance section of the *Daily Telegraph.*

'Not all planners are dodgy, Dad. I've known Ben for 25 years and he's an incredibly successful adviser, with a string of letters after his name.'

'Well, I think you better put the girls in after-school care for an extra day,' said her dad. Jayne was surprised. Her parents never said no when she asked for help, and this was for a very good reason. But her dad continued. 'We'll go with you. I want to check this guy out for myself. Besides, it makes sense if we make a plan together, don't you think?' he asked, to the surprise of Jayne.

'Your mum and I aren't going to keep this house forever, and perhaps it's time we looked at how we could move onto the next phase of our life.'

Jayne absorbed what her dad was saying with quiet joy. She wasn't in this alone. She was incredibly lucky to have the parents she did — always supporting her, never abandoning their grown daughter and grandchildren. She knew so many other single mums who weren't as lucky.

'Sure, Dad, I'll let you know what time I get in,' she said with a smile in her voice. She put down the phone and turned back to the wispy hair. With a flourish and her super-strength hair spray, she sprayed the girls' hair flat. 'Nobody light a match,' she laughed as the girls spluttered under a cloud of fumes. They both looked in the mirror and obviously liked what they saw. They launched themselves on Jayne for a monster cuddle. Jayne happily cuddled them back while trying to keep the hair intact. Life really was good.

***

Across town, Brad was wrangling a different kind of challenge. Eyeing his phone, he was mentally preparing himself to call his mother. Knowing that she had cancer and wouldn't be around forever had changed everything for him — mainly because he was smart enough to know a lot of unfinished business still festered between him and his parents. With a sharp outtake of breath, he dialled his parents' number. His dad picked up on the second ring. 'It's me, Dad,' said Brad quickly, before he lost his nerve. 'Are you guys up for an early dinner?'

Brad's dad replied quickly. 'Sure, son, where do you want us to meet you?'

'I'll come to you,' was Brad's response.

His father went silent for a moment, and then said, 'I'm not sure your mum will feel up to cooking, Brad.'

Knowing what he did, he immediately felt a pang of sorrow. 'That's fine, I'll bring some Chinese takeout,' he said, and hung up before the conversation could go any further. He rang the building concierge and asked for Chinese for three to be organised, knowing nothing was a problem in these apartments. He then texted his driver to pick him up in 20 minutes.

In the meantime, he couldn't help himself drifting back to thinking about Josie. He Googled her name and found a particularly ravishing image of her beside a large story on influential women in Australia from a leading business magazine. The woman was stunning — more than that, though, she was real.

Last night had been one of the best nights Brad had had in a long time. For once, he felt part of something. Not at the lead, but part of a group of equals. It felt good to confide in friends. He hadn't realised how much he'd missed that.

He closed his laptop and reflected on what Ben had revealed to him about his mum. *It's time to put things right*, he thought to himself as he left the building and went downstairs to collect the Chinese, and to confront his past. It was going to be an interesting evening.

# Chapter 18

# **Reality bites**

Ben smiled each time he received another message from one of his friends from the reunion asking for an appointment. He knew they could benefit from advice, but even he hadn't thought all of them would act on this so quickly. He had his EA shuffle his week around so he could fit them all in. No time like the present to act. He knew the longer they waited, the easier it would be to stay stuck in their present ways.

First in his diary was Josephine, and he was looking forward to hearing more about her business and how she had set up her financial affairs.

Josephine arrived at his office five minutes early, looking immaculate as always. She shook his hand warmly and sat down in the chair opposite him. From her poise, it was hard to tell what she was thinking. Ben knew she was used to the pace of corporate life, so he dispensed with the usual chitchat and cut straight to the chase.

'Why don't you tell me about how your company is set up—things like ownership structure, debt, free cash flow and profit lines,' Ben said.

Josephine smiled, and pulled her iPad out of her bag. She was ready for these sorts of questions, and was soon showing Ben her financial accounts for the past few years, an organisational structure chart, and how she managed her cash flow via a sophisticated Excel spreadsheet.

Ben was impressed. She knew her business very well — including its strengths and weakness. It was a very profitable enterprise. He could also see very large chunks of cash were taken out from the financials every year as dividends to Josie.

'Let's look at the free cash flow in your personal life,' said Ben, and here Josie hesitated. The number of investment properties she had, and the lifestyle she lived, meant that she needed a considerable amount of cash to come out of her business, and into the rest of her life.

She tapped on a folder titled Properties, and outlined the various properties she had either an interest in or was the sole owner of. He could see from the types of properties that this was a high-quality property portfolio indeed. He asked Josie how much debt was across all properties, and she revealed it was several million dollars in total.

With the negative gearing coming from renting them out, Josie's property strategy made sense on paper. But an enormous amount of cash was required to keep all the properties ticking over, including paying off the mortgages and managing agent costs and repairs and maintenance. While she had a successful business, Ben knew immediately that she was holding too much property in her overall investment portfolio. And maintaining the debt was causing some stress.

Ben asked Josie which property was her favourite. Outside of her Paddington terrace where she lived, Josie loved her heritage farmhouse in Bowral best of all. If it wasn't rented out, she went there occasionally to clear her head. Ben looked at the debt on this property versus the others, and asked Josie how many others she would need to sell to be able to pay this one off outright.

Josie looked at her portfolio and did the mental maths. If she sold off the Hunter Valley winery stake she had and the remaining two properties, she could most likely own this.

Ben then asked about her business. Why was she still the only shareholder? Josie paused for a moment before she spoke. 'To be honest, I've never really trusted anyone else. I like to be in control,' she admitted. Ben nodded in understanding. So many business owners he worked with felt the same way. But by controlling everything they were also taking on all the risk and stress of the business. They didn't have an equal to share the load.

Ben asked about Josie's team. Did she have others who could join the leadership ranks? Would anyone be interested in buying into the business?

Josie stopped for a moment to consider her staff members. Both her Account Director and her GM could possibly afford to buy a stake in the business. She definitely wanted to keep them on the team.

Ben went on to talk about the benefits of a part management buyout, explaining how this would tie key members of the team into the financial success of the business, and how it meant all the responsibility did not need to rest on her.

'It's also the first step in a real succession plan,' continued Ben, explaining to Josie how building a real succession plan for her to capitalise on the asset she had built might take five to seven years.

Josie could see where Ben was going. Her getting her business ready for sale over the longer term made a lot more sense than just keeping on as she had. She knew she was getting tired and, while five years seemed an eternity away, she also knew that good things took time—building the business had taken her almost two decades, after all.

Ben asked a few more questions about her personal spending, and where the majority of her spending went. Josie outlined the costs for her wardrobe, hair, make-up and five-star travel every year, and then suddenly broke off laughing. 'God! I'm a total high-maintenance cliché,' she giggled as Ben smiled at her confession.

Josie thought back to Ben's unlearning money circle from the gym. Desire was definitely the top of her list when it came to unlearning money.

'I'm not going to tell you what not to spend. You're more than capable of figuring that out for yourself,' said Ben. 'What I am going to tell you is this. If you continue to spend at this rate, you're going to need to keep working at the same rate. Now, from what I have heard, it sounds like you are getting a little tired. And that's totally normal for someone who has worked consistently for more than 20 years building up a business. Do you want to keep working at the same pace?' he asked with his head tipped to one side.

Josie thought for a moment and then visibly sank into her chair. Her very body language spoke of how tired she was. She shook her head and smiled sadly at Ben. Needing to slow down wasn't easy to admit, and Ben knew this was hard for Josie to accept and face. She had set her life up in a certain way, and he was questioning pretty much every facet of it.

'Now is the hardest part—and it will get easier,' said Ben, as he explained that most people wanted to reinvent their lives at this age. The realisation that it couldn't be done instantly, however, was pretty demotivating. He went on to explain how he and his team could put together a long-term financial plan for Josie. This would include consolidating her property debt, investing any free cash flow and helping her set up the right corporate structures to sell down at least a part of her business.

Josie nodded while Ben outlined the components of his plan. She knew it would take several years for this plan to take full effect, but the sooner she started, the sooner she could transition. She gave Ben a hug, and thanked him for being a catalyst in her life.

'How do I pay you?' she asked, almost as an afterthought.

Ben asked Josie what would work for her. Having a business, she was used to paying invoices, and so she asked Ben to charge her for the advice given. She also asked what it would cost to go on a monthly maintenance retainer. Ben knew it made more sense for him to charge the fee with some follow-up hours included, and explained how his firm charged and the kind of cost she could expect. Including her business advice, she was looking at a total of around $6000 for the first year. Not a problem for someone of Josie's income level.

They both looked at their diaries and set up another time to meet in three weeks, when the formal advice would be presented. Josie formed a mental list in her head of things she wanted to consider in the meantime. They included getting updated valuations on all her properties, and talking to her key staff members about the possibility of buying in. As well as her day-to-day activities, this would keep her more than busy. She was used to using her time efficiently and knew she would fit it in. She had a skip in her step as she left Ben's office and headed for her car.

She felt more energised than she had in a long time. Having a plan and the ability to reinvent what her life would look like was exciting. The only thing missing now was love.

The image of the kiss she shared with Brad filled her mind and, for a moment, she let herself get lost in it. With everything she had going on, now wasn't an ideal time to pursue an international romance. But the thought of not seeing Brad again left her cold. If a chance existed to explore their feelings further, Josie knew in her heart she would take it—no matter the cost. You couldn't put a price on finding the one. Nobody else in her life had made her feel the way Brad had. She just hoped he felt the same way.

*** 

Meanwhile, the reality of Brad's life was hitting him in a very different way. He sat across the table from his parents, sharing the excellent Chinese food and watching his mother's face intently, looking for signs of the illness he knew she had.

Her skin was sallow—he didn't know why he hadn't noticed that yellowish tinge when he saw her before the reunion. She had bags under her eyes, but that was pretty normal. In Brad's mind, his mother always looked harried and tired.

As his mother prattled on about how she was annoyed that the school reunion story hadn't appeared in the paper today, Brad felt his frustration rising. Was this woman ever going to come clean with him? As her son, didn't he deserve the truth?

Brad looked at his father. His dad was listening to his mother intently, like she was saying something of utmost importance. In the end, it was that look that made Brad snap.

'While we waste time talking yet again about nothing, you fail to tell me the real news, mother,' he said coldly. His mother stopped her story and looked at her son, shocked.

'What do you mean? The real news?' she asked, a little timidly.

His father's face looked worried, but Brad didn't back down.

'The news that you have cancer, Mum,' said Brad harshly, and the room fell silent for a moment, broken by his mother.

'Who told you?' she cried angrily. 'My health is nobody else's business.'

Brad stared at her in disbelief. Anger was not how he'd expected her to react. Then again, when did she ever behave like a normal person? Brad stabbed a won ton from his soup and then stared into his mother's eyes. 'It doesn't matter who told me, Mother, what matters is that you didn't.'

At that, his mother fell silent again and her face fell. She knew she had let her son down by allowing him to find out she was sick from someone else.

Surprisingly, it was Brad's father who spoke up. 'What would you have done if your mum had told you, Brad? Sent flowers? Bought her a wing at the hospital? Quite frankly, you give your mother no time, so actually getting the time to tell you something important like this wasn't exactly easy.'

Brad was stunned. His father had rarely spoken this frankly to him as a man. While they had clashed many times when he was a teenager, it had now been a long time since they had exchanged harsh words. In fact, they rarely exchanged many words at all.

Brad started to feel uneasy. He'd gotten so used to the resentment he felt at his parents for everything they'd pushed him into when he was growing up, he had little else to fall back on in the feelings and relationship department when it came to them.

It seemed, however, that they had a few resentments of their own.

'What are you saying, Dad, that I'm a bad son?' Brad responded in a tight voice.

His mother looked up alarmed. She hated a scene and she could sense that this conversation could escalate at any second.

'I didn't want to worry you, Brad. I know how busy you are, how important your work is.'

Brad was even more shocked. Did his mother actually think he was too busy to hear about her cancer? But he had a sinking feeling in his stomach as he thought back on the past few years. The blow-off phone calls, the presents bought by his assistant and the fleeting visits he always resented having to do. He guessed communicating something as important as this over the phone may not have been easy for his mother.

'But were you ever going to tell me?' Brad asked but in a less angry tone. Her mother shook her head. 'I didn't want to distract you or worry you. You are far too important to worry about me.'

Her statement ended with her eyes starting to get glassy as she held back tears. His father took her hand and squeezed it gently for support.

'As usual, Brad, your mother puts you first. Always before herself.'

Brad looked surprised. 'I'm not sure I would say that is usual.' More than a little bitterness had leaked into his voice. 'If you said to me she pushed me, obsessed over me, demanded of me, I might have related. But putting me first? It's never really felt like that.'

Brad's father's chair exploded into the wall as he stood up from the table. 'You selfish bastard,' he spat at Brad. 'You think your mother pushed you for her own benefit? We gave up everything to get you where you are today. The price was a big one, and it included your mother's health.' His mother tugged on Brad's father's sleeve to make him sit down. But he was just getting started.

'How the hell do you think you got to where you are? We pushed you because we knew you had talent. And you whined and whinged every step of the goddamn way. Do you think your mother enjoyed getting up at 4 am every day to take you to swim practice? Do you think the hours of study she put in helping you at school made her life better? How about the holidays we didn't take because we didn't want to ruin your routine? Everything was about you. And look at you now. It was worth it. You've achieved beyond most people's wildest dreams. You just never grew up enough to admit who helped you get there.' With that, his father's shoulders slumped and he sank back in his chair, and put his head in his hands.

Brad was shocked. He had never heard his father speak this way. More than that, he had never considered that's how they felt about him. He let this truth sink in for a moment, before he trusted himself to speak. When he did, he felt his voice waver a little.

'I guess you're right, Dad,' he admitted. 'I never did stop to think about the toll it would take on both of you. Especially Mum.'

'It's alright, Brad, I only ever wanted the best for you,' his mother quickly interjected. He looked at her in amazement.

Suddenly his world spun as he considered that everything he thought about his childhood might be wrong. He'd believed he had been unreasonably pushed and used as a trophy. Instead, he was starting to see the sacrifice his parents made to get him to great heights. This realisation made his heart ache. He had wasted so many years resenting and avoiding the people who had loved him more than anyone. His father was right. He was selfish.

He stood up and went around to his mother's side of the table. He took her hand and pulled her into a hug. He said nothing, but let his chin rest on her head as he held her tight. Her body felt thin and frail, and he suddenly felt afraid.

'What sort of cancer is it, Mum?' he whispered as he hugged her. His mother's body started to rack with sobs, and she continued to hold him tight, saying nothing.

'It's stomach cancer, Brad, and there's nothing more that can be done,' his father said quietly, eyes full of sadness as he watched his wife in his son's arms. He was devastated that a moment like this had only come because of a terminal illness.

'We shall see about that,' said Brad in a determined voice, thinking of all the people he knew in science and medicine around the world. Surely someone could help his mother.

His mother shook her head sadly. 'There's nothing you can do, sweetheart. When my time is up, it's up.' She set her shoulders back and assumed her usual tough demeanour. 'You just focus on your work. You're doing some incredible things. Don't worry about your old mum. I've had my life.'

She'd chosen not to go through another round of chemo. She'd already done that and, when the cancer came back, she knew she'd had enough. She wanted to spend what time she had left out of hospitals and treatment centres. Her family had grown up and she'd achieved what she wanted to. Nobody needed her anymore. Of course, her husband would be lost without her. But he would go on. They had lots of friends and support.

Brad sensed that his mother didn't have much time left at all. His heart felt heavy and his head pounded. He needed some air, and some time to think.

He stood up and gave both his parents a hug. 'I'll be back in the morning. I just need to organise a few things,' he said, as he cleared up the takeaway containers from the table.

'Leave that, son,' his father said kindly, seeing the stress on Brad's face. 'We'll see you tomorrow.'

Brad left their home with a heavy heart and headed back to his apartment. He couldn't face this alone and he needed someone to talk to. Before he knew what he was doing, he was dialling Josie's number. She picked up on the second ring.

'You free?' he asked.

'Sure, come over,' she said immediately. She texted him her address and his car made its way through the evening traffic toward her home.

She opened the door in jeans and a T-shirt and he felt a wave of relief wash over him when he saw her.

He picked her up in a hug, and she looked surprised. 'I did only see you two days ago,' she laughed, but was pleased. She grabbed his hand and led him down the hallway into her lounge room. It was full of white flowers and candles, and was one of the most elegant and inviting rooms Brad had seen.

He sank onto her overstuffed couch, and proceeded to fill her in on everything that had happened at his parents' place. Josie whistled softly. 'Holy cow, Brad. I had no idea your parents thought like that.'

As Brad's girlfriend in high school, she had seen firsthand the pressure Brad had on him to succeed. She had been in agreement with him that his parents were overbearing. Yet, she had to admit, they had gotten a pretty amazing result. Brad was exceptional. He had built an incredible empire, and was doing work that could actually change the world for the better. And she knew he must now be going through hell. No matter how much he had resented his mum, knowing that she wouldn't be around for much longer, and how hard she'd worked for his success, was a heavy burden.

'What do you want to do about it?' she asked him, throwing her leg over his on the couch. It was an intimate moment, and anyone walking in who didn't know them would swear they had been married for 20 years.

'I don't know, but I need time to find out,' he answered and then made his mind up. He would base his headquarters out of Sydney for the next month. His EA would have a heart attack in trying to change his diary around, but he knew that he owed his parents his time — while his mother was still physically able. He also knew it would give him a month to spend time with Josie, and explore what they had together.

Josie received this news with a happy heart. While it was a hard time for Brad with his mum being so sick, the thought of spending time with him over the next month was incredible. Who knew what would happen after that? For the moment, however, it was more than enough.

She snuggled into his chest and held him tight. What he needed now was support, and she was more than willing to give it. When she looked up into his eyes, she saw the face of the boy she had loved in high school — uncertain and worried. She got up and took his hand, leading him into her bedroom.

She pulled off her T-shirt and slipped off her jeans, while he stood there silently. She then pulled out his shirt and tugged at his buttons. With little effort, he picked her up and placed her gently on the enormous white bed. He slid off his jeans and lay next to her. He was gentle and loving. It would be their first night together in more than 20 years, yet it felt as familiar as yesterday. Josie smiled to herself as she turned off the lamp. Hard as it could be, life could also be good.

# Chapter 19

# New ventures

Karen had a washing basket on one hip and her mobile at her ear, holding it with her shoulder. She was on the phone to the head of the P&C, in the middle of asking if she could take out some space in the school newsletter next month.

Luckily, this woman was a fan and she quickly agreed to support the promotion of Karen's new website. She was, after all, one of the most hard-working mothers in the school—always volunteering, baking, crafting and fundraising. Karen had worked tirelessly at the primary school throughout her children's attendance there. Now, at Russ's suggestion, she was calling in the favour and asking for some support.

Nate had assured her the website would be ready to populate next week. She had spent the past three days writing down everything she knew—about everything. Bella had looked at all her thoughts, and started to categorise them into areas such as kitchen, bathroom, laundry and school. She had also begun the process of taking quirky pictures on her iPhone to go next to the individual tips. Karen had to admit, it was going to look amazing.

She was going to meet Russ at Ben's office after lunch, and quickly threw the load of washing on and went to comb her hair. She was excited to tell Ben about the progress she had made already on her business idea and hastily grabbed her coat from the back of the door to walk out. She walked back to check her image in the mirror and her usual 'mum' style stared back at her. Just a lip gloss and tinted moisturiser; hair pulled back in a ponytail. She threw back her shoulders and made herself a promise. Once she turned a profit, she was going to give herself a makeover—after all, new business, new future, new Karen. She was excited.

Pulling up her station wagon in Ben's parking lot, she saw Russ get out of a cab. She walked over and gave him an excited hug—Russ grinned back. He loved seeing Karen so happy. He realised how long it had been since he had seen her consistently at this level of energy.

They walked into Ben's office hand in hand and waited in reception. Ben soon came to greet them and took them into a meeting room. On the whiteboard were magnetic figurines of people. It all looked a little bit like kindergarten and Karen was intrigued.

Once the pleasantries were out of the way, Karen saw Russ clear his throat and adjust his tie nervously. She knew his body language well enough to know what he was about to say made him uncomfortable.

'Mate, before we start, can I ask how much this advice will cost? It's not that we don't value you. It's just that we never found out exactly what it would cost.'

Ben understood. In fact he was more than used to that being the first question new clients asked him.

'Everyone's different, and some people like Josie have business needs as well as personal, which moves the dial on cost. But for couples with a family, we have a retainer model. For $200 per month we can review your insurances, do your wills and estate planning, and put together a financial plan and be able to touch base with you on a regular basis.

Russ sighed in relief. This was a much better cost structure than he'd expected, and he knew Karen could definitely juggle

$200 bucks a month—even it meant not going out for a meal or two.

Ben then asked them did they have a will prepared, and had they thought about what would happen to the kids if either of them passed away.

'My parents would take the kids if something happened to us,' Karen said quickly, realising that while that was the assumed plan, nothing had been formally set up.

Ben went to the board and moved the magnetic people around. He asked them to name all the people in their extended family who were important to them. Karen listed her parents and cousins. Russ put down his mum and brother.

Ben asked if they were in agreement with Karen's parents getting custody should anything happen. Russ nodded. He knew his mother was too old to cope with three kids and his brother was recently divorced. He was definitely not in a position to do anything.

As they started talking more about this, Ben started asking them to visualise the unthinkable. What would happen to their income if Russ died? How much were they insured for? Russ knew he had a million dollars in insurance through his super fund, and assured Ben that was covered.

But Ben started to dig deeper on that. 'How much is your mortgage?' he asked. When Karen told him it was $700 000, he wrote that figure on the board. 'And school fees, living expenses per month, just the necessities?'

When Karen listed out the $17 000 per year in school fees for two of the kids, and the $5000 per month in living costs, Russ was quick to see that his initial statement on his $1 million insurance policy was far from right. Some quick sums told him his living costs outside of the mortgage were $94k per year. So a million dollar payout might allow Karen to pay off the mortgage, but the remaining $200k would be pretty quickly eaten up in a couple years. She would need to make a lot more money to see the kids through to university.

Ben told them not to worry. He would assess the insurance cover they currently had and then get his team to do some analysis on the most cost-effective way to cover all their costs if something were to happen. He also wanted to put a cost to Russ if Karen died—after all, someone had to be the primary carer for the kids and, most likely, Russ would need to put a full-time nanny on to be able to continue in his job if the worst did happen.

All this talk was starting to put Karen on a downer. She had come here to talk about her new plan for an online business with Ben, and instead he was asking them to picture death, tragedy and worse-case scenarios. This wasn't exactly inspiring stuff.

Ben sensed the mood had changed, and instantly addressed the elephant in the room. 'Guys, nobody wants to think of the worst—it's human nature to stay away from pain. But if you get to see one thing in my job, it's what can happen to people when they don't have a plan. By going through this now, and putting up with a bit of discomfort in talking through these scenarios, we can put a plan in place. Then you can forget all about it. But let me tell you—I know from personal experience that you will sleep a little more soundly at night, knowing that if you have a crisis, you have a plan, and money won't be what you are stressing about.'

Ben's words made sense and Russ nodded in agreement. He actually felt guilty that he'd never looked at this before. He worked in finance, for goodness sake. He should have been more prepared. Ben assured them both that it was pretty normal to get to your forties and not have these bases covered. He was happy that he was able to take care of them now. It was one reason he loved what he did.

He talked them through getting a power of attorney done for each of them, so the other could legally make decisions in a situation where it was needed. He also looked at putting in a policy for income protection if Russ was injured and couldn't do the same job, or if the kids got sick and they needed time off work to look after them.

Ben then quickly moved on to ask them both about the future. With the key risks taken care of, they could focus on how they wanted to reinvent their lives.

Karen sat up straighter, jumping in to tell Ben about her new business idea. While she didn't have the full picture of what exactly she was going to sell on the site, she did know that if she could build a big enough community around her ideas, she could find a way to commercialise them. Ben nodded in approval. As long as she wasn't spending a lot of their free cash flow on the idea, and it could fit in around her already busy schedule, he knew she could make a success of it.

Russ talked about his work, explaining how he really wanted to make a move, but he knew that if he started a new gig, he would have to put in the hours to get up to speed in a different industry from what he was used to. 'I've made the decision to stay put for a while,' he said. Karen looked at him in surprise. She knew he really was excited about the prospect of changing jobs, and this was not what she'd expected to hear.

But Russ had really thought it through. 'Babe, I want to give you the chance to really build this thing. I can do more around the house, and I can also probably organise to work from home one day a week — that way, I can do pick-ups and sports drop-offs, and give you more time to get your website off the ground.

Karen couldn't believe what she was hearing. Russ wanted to share the load! She squeezed his hand so tight she could hear knuckles crack. This was more than she could ever have expected. She knew Russ had a big job and a lot of pressure. That he would put more priority on her, despite his load, and not move to something else was incredibly selfless. She had married a damn good man.

Ben thought what Russ had said made perfect sense, and congratulated him on being strategic enough to see a bigger picture. While it meant in the short term changes would be made for Karen, Russ staying put and holding down the fort gave them time to see if they could diversify their income elsewhere.

Ben also urged them to think further ahead to what their life could look like when the kids grew up. Would they stay in Sydney and downsize their house? Or would they move somewhere cheaper and use the profit on the house to boost up their super? What age did they want to retire at?

Ben looked at the current super documents Russ had brought in. He looked at the cost of the fund and the attached insurances, and said he thought he could get them a better deal. He promised to come back with some recommendations on their super as well.

While Ben and Karen didn't have all the answers, it was exciting to start thinking about it.

Finally, they went through the process of cash flow. Ben showed them a spreadsheet that he wanted them to start filling out together at home. In it were lists of items that were a possible monthly cost to the family—including everything from Netflix subscriptions to mobile phone and wireless costs. Ben knew putting all the costs together would take them a bit of time, but things like water bills, electricity and rates all added up. And many times people were more than a little surprised to see how much things cost when it was all down. Once they had that information, they could set up a way to put an amount aside for savings that could represent the start of an emergency 'buffer fund'. This fund was typically three months' salary, which could be used if desperately needed.

Ben went on to explain that having this buffer was another way to get a better sleep. The fund meant they would have enough money to buy some time if the worst happened. Without that buffer, Karen would have to keep juggling to make ends meet—and, if Russ lost his job, it would be a disaster the way their finances were currently. Ben thought it might take a couple of years to save the buffer—but you had to start somewhere, and they were moving in the right direction.

At the end of the meeting, Ben looked them both in the eye. 'Congratulations. You've just taken the first step to making sure you get what you want out of life in the long term. I'm proud of you both.'

Karen hugged him and Russ clapped his shoulder affectionately. 'Mate, you are a game changer for us,' he said, knowing how important this meeting was, and how it had given them the ability to really plan for their future together. 'We will be forever grateful.'

They made another time to come back in three weeks to see the details of phase one of their plan. They also promised Ben that they would talk more about their future, so he could start to help them cost out longer term life planning as well.

They left the office and decided to go to the bar across the road and have a wine to celebrate. Life was good. It felt like a new beginning. Ben was someone they could trust and, while it wouldn't be an overnight transformation, they could both see it was the start of something different. They were feeling like they were creating a life with more intention, rather than living year to year as they had been. Karen also ordered hot chips from the bar and mentally absolved herself from the carbs. After all, she was celebrating.

# Chapter 20

# Change of fortune

Jayne was nervous as she drove with her parents to Ben's office. Her father could be bloody rude at times, and she knew he would grill Ben about his true intentions. He'd made it clear he didn't trust 'dodgy' financial advisers, and would be there to look out for her as much as anything.

'Remember, Dad, Ben is a friend. Please don't embarrass me and ask lots of suspicious questions,' Jayne warned her father, looking at him in the rear-view mirror as she parked the car.

Her mother adjusted her lipstick in the sun visor mirror, and also gave her father the evil eye. 'Yes, don't embarrass us, Bob.'

Jayne's father looked innocent as he opened the car door—which Jayne knew didn't mean much. When Jayne introduced him to Ben, however, he was perfectly behaved, and she started to relax. This was a mistake.

'Our Jayne says good things about you,' he told Ben, who smiled. He then went on. 'But she's not the best judge of character when it comes to men. So I'd like to know more about you myself.'

Jayne gasped and her mother kicked her husband under the table. Ben, of course, handled it perfectly. 'Bob, I'm an open book,' he replied. 'Ask away.'

'Alright, I will,' replied Bob pulling a piece of paper from his pocket. 'What qualification do you have to be giving advice?' asked Bob.

Ben pointed to a framed certificate on the wall. 'I'm a CFP qualified adviser, with a degree in economics.' Bob nodded to hear this. He had read on the Financial Planning Association website that CFP qualified advisers were recognised as the most highly qualified.

'Who are you licensed with?' grilled Bob. Ben went on to explain he was independently licensed, and worked only on a fee-for-service basis. He didn't make commissions on selling financial products, and was only paid for the advice he and his colleagues gave.

This seemed to appease Bob, who sat back meekly and turned to Jayne. 'Go on,' he urged, and she gave him a withering look. While she didn't mind her father asking questions, she did resent the comment about her not being a good judge of character. That was a low blow, even if her ex-husband didn't represent the finest example of her judgement.

Jayne quickly outlined the conversation she'd had with Ben at the reunion. She knew her financial position was precarious to say the least, and was keen to get on the right path — not only for the girls' sake, but also for her own peace of mind. She didn't want to be retired and poor. Ben asked her about her salary and super contribution. When Jayne told him it was $90 000 plus the minimum 9.5 per cent super, her mother's ears pricked up.

'I thought you were on more than that Jayne. Good God — you have a law degree.'

Jayne turned to her mother in surprise. 'Mum, I work part-time. I'm in-house counsel because I can only work limited hours with the girls. It's not a bad salary for part-time.'

Ben agreed that for part-time work the salary wasn't bad, but he did point out that at this level she couldn't afford to save enough super for her retirement. People were living much longer now, and rather than retiring at 65 and living until 70, people had to think about working much longer and most likely living into their eighties and nineties.

Ben then turned to Jayne's parents. 'Bob, Cath, I know Jayne is your only child. Do you intend to leave her a legacy?'

'Absolutely,' said Bob. 'We intend on leaving Jayne our house. We paid $48 000 for it back in the day, and it's now worth well over $1.8 million.'

Ben smiled as he looked at them. 'That's great, but you both look pretty fit. I don't see you keeling over any time soon. So I don't see Jayne getting her hands on that property anytime in the next 10 years—leaving her aged at least 55 with relatively little savings and the girls going off to university.'

Jayne stared at the table. When Ben put things like this, it made her feel afraid. Reaching 55 with no real way to pay for retirement, let alone buy a house, terrified her. This was not the meeting she was hoping for. Instead of making a plan that allowed her to have more, Ben was pointing out that she had little hope of getting ahead.

Ben touched her arm and smiled reassuringly. 'I only ask these questions of your parents because they clearly love you, and probably haven't been presented with options for helping you sooner than when they pass away.'

Both Bob and Cath listened on with interest. Ben was sure right about that.

Ben then went on to outline how many parents were now selling their homes earlier. They were making decisions about downsizing, and freeing up the excess capital to give to their children—either to buy a property or to invest in their super to give them time to benefit from 25 years of compounding interest.

'I don't want to make Mum and Dad leave their home. That's the house I had my whole childhood in. We couldn't let that go.'

'Who said so?' said Jayne's mother defiantly. 'To be honest, I'm sick to death of cleaning a house that size. And your father is always whinging about doing the lawns and the gardens.'

Bob started to protest at the whinging part, but then shut his mouth. He was sick of the mowing, that was the truth.

Ben outlined how they could have their house valued, and also take the time to do things up around the place, to make sure they got the best possible price. The market was strong and they lived in a good area. They weren't in a rush—unlike so many people when selling the family home. Those who didn't plan usually ended up having to sell to fund a retirement home, and that wasn't always the ideal time to maximise a sale.

Ben also outlined a number of areas that had good retirement villages, offering homes with new style and fantastic facilities, social activities and even pools and gymnasiums. He could help them find some options that were affordable, and didn't lock them in with unreasonable contracts. Cath started to look excited, and even Bob had a small smile on his face.

Jayne realised the opportunity she would be given if her parents decided to take this step. While she would have liked to own a house one day, she was happy in the unit with the girls. It was a new building, and she felt safe. But the thought of having a superannuation fund that was ticking over with a good amount felt amazing.

'To live on $80 000 a year for life after you retire, assuming you live into your eighties, will take about $2 million,' said Ben. Jayne knew what she'd need was a lot, but had never stopped to figure out just how much. She knew without a doubt that, unless she met someone with money or her parents did help, she would never have enough to be self-funded.

'There's always the pension, Ben,' said Bob, who received some pension benefits as a retiree.

'Bob, there will only be 2.7 people working for every retired person when Karen is 70. There simply won't be enough taxpayers in Australia to support the current system.'

Bob looked shocked at this, and took Cath's hand. 'My wife and I have some talking to do, Ben,' he said.

Ben went on to ask Jayne about her current super fund and insurance arrangements. Jayne admitted she didn't even have insurance, and Ben wanted to get this fixed ASAP. 'If something happened to you, your parents would need the funds to raise the girls, if your ex didn't step up. We need to get that sorted.'

Jayne agreed. She knew she couldn't count on the girls' father. This meeting had been full of revelations and none of them particularly good. She hadn't realised just how much was at stake. Ben also urged Jayne to look around the job market.

'You're a clever woman and you could earn more. Put a higher value on yourself. I have no doubt you have the ability.'

Jayne was about to make the usual protests that the girls came first, and she could only work part-time. It was her mother who then spoke up. 'Jayne, we could get the girls to school every day if we needed to, and pick them up if they're not in after-school care. We love them and know how good it would be for them and you if you were able to earn more.'

Jayne started to think about the possibilities, and the kind of law she used to dream of practising. And she started wondering what those jobs would pay. She had some investigating to do.

Ben finished up the meeting by saying he would be able to put Jayne on a $100 a month retainer to do all the insurance, super, budgeting and wills. He would give advice for her parents on structuring their legacy for a one-off $1600 fee. This seemed reasonable on both counts, and not even Bob complained.

The three of them left Ben's office with a lot to think about. All this planning meant change and, while it was most likely necessary, it would take some getting used to. Luckily, they had no pressing emergency to deal with — they had the time and space to really think it through and lean on Ben and his advice.

Jayne dropped her parents back home and went to pick up the girls from after-school care. She would start looking at new jobs tonight. She was determined to change her fortunes before it was too late. She owed it to her girls.

Both girls jumped in the car after she'd signed them out, fighting and pulling each other's hair. Jayne sighed as she headed home. Sometimes parenting could be extremely frustrating. 'Girls, if you don't fight, I'll let you play your iPads after dinner,' she bribed. They both sat up straight and behaved instantly. The lure of the screen worked again. While Jayne wished she had a more wholesome pursuit to get them to behave, she used the thing they would value the most. She knew her children well.

# Chapter 21
# The coach

Jasper sat nervously in Ben's office waiting to go in. He had his mother with him, who had dressed up for the occasion in almost every piece of jewellery that she owned. Jasper thought that she was trying to look like she had lots of money—although why you would want to look wealthy to the person who you needed money advice from was beyond him!

Ben came out and greeted them both with a firm handshake. Jasper introduced his mother with a wink. Ben gave her a warm smile. 'Lovely to meet you, Isobel,' he said. 'You have quite a son.'

'Tell me about it,' she replied drily, and Jasper winced.

They walked into Ben's office, and his mother looked around the room curiously. 'Do you know David Koch from *Sunrise*?' she asked.

'No, I'm afraid I don't, Isobel,' Ben replied solemnly.

'He knows an awful lot about finance. I expect you would listen to him. And Ross Greenwood on Channel 9.'

'They are commentators, Mum, not advisers,' said Jasper for at least the tenth time that week. He had asked her not to bring it up in front of Ben—and it was the first thing that came out of her mouth.

'They are very popular, I know,' said Ben reassuringly. Many clients he saw took what they read in the papers and saw on TV as the gospel. What they had never done, usually, was get specific financial advice for their situation. Jasper's mother seemed pleased with Ben's response, and sat back in her chair. She was very interested to see what Jasper was going to tell Ben. His plans to go back to university surprised and delighted her, but she had to wonder whether he would actually go through with them.

Jasper cleared his throat and started the conversation. 'I think you were right the other night, Ben. It's probably time I did something that I'm actually half decent at, and the thought of being a coach or PE teacher is pretty damn appealing. I think I should go back to school.'

Ben was genuinely pleased for Jasper. While it would be tough to get into the routine of study, he knew that Jasper could entirely reinvent his life into his fifties, and have a rewarding career for up to 20 years at least. Something he would never regret doing.

He talked to Jasper about possible options for mature age study, part-time versus full-time, and how his Higher Education Contribution debt could be delayed until he started working.

He also got Jasper to think about what his income would look like. He most likely couldn't do his current sales job while studying. Could he do something at night, or around the course so he could still earn money while learning?

Jasper said he would look around, and his mother looked at him squarely in the eye. 'A developer offered me $800 000 to subdivide our yard. It's a massive backyard, and nobody uses it. It would be great if we could get that money now, and it helped you study.'

Jasper looked at his mother in amazement. 'Why are you only telling me this now?'

'Because I didn't want you getting your hands on that money and blowing it,' his mother replied with her usual blunt honesty.

Jasper looked offended, and Ben smiled awkwardly. 'Sounds like lots of changes are going on in your lives, and that's positive. Tough to deal with, perhaps, but very much worthwhile.'

Jasper's mother nodded slowly. She hadn't intended to blurt out the news on the developer that way. In fact, she was thinking of just rejecting the offer without even telling Jasper. That backyard had been her husband's pride and joy. His vegetable patch and tool shed were still in pride of place, and that would all have to go if it was subdivided into a battleaxe block.

She knew, however, that Jasper desperately needed this chance to reinvent himself. If that money was available, and she could still keep her house, maybe he could buy himself a one-bedroom unit with the rest.

She outlined this idea to Ben, who listened carefully. When she concluded, he took out his pen and started scribbling notes. In a moment he looked up and cleared his throat.

'If today has taught us one thing, it's that you never know what's going to happen in the future. Jasper needs some money over the next three to four years to be able to study and still live. He is also going to need a big boost to his super for retirement. I don't think putting the money into a unit is going to be the best strategy for him. He needs some liquidity to be able to use money now — investing some inside super and outside super in low-risk investments would suit him better.'

Isobel knew nothing about investing in shares and other things. She only knew property. While she was worried that Jasper might lose the money, she also could see that Ben knew what he was talking about. His office was nicely furnished and in a good part of town. He was obviously successful at his work.

'I'd like to know more about that, but am open to whatever will give Jasper the right result,' she said, smiling at her son. Jasper was speechless. Suddenly an $800 000 windfall was in the offing, and he may actually get to have a career that he was proud of. Unbelievable.

Ben asked Jasper to list all the places he'd worked, so he could start tracking down his super. It would be in several different funds, and he would be paying fees on them all. Finding the funds would also tell Ben what his insurance would look like. It was important to get Jasper in the right low-cost fund, get some insurance on his income and put a plan together to use some of this new windfall for retirement savings, to start building the super Jasper would need when he did eventually retire. While he would earn super as a teacher, the 20 years at 9.5 per cent of a salary most likely between $70 000 and $90 000 would not be enough to retire comfortably.

Isobel wanted help dealing with the property developer, and Ben offered to do that too. He had a fair bit of experience in these sorts of negotiations and was happy to take part. He also knew Isobel would need a valuation of her home after the sale of the land, and a plan for what she would do when she eventually wanted to go into aged care. While she was at least 10 years away from that if her health remained, having a plan in place and some idea of the money involved was still a good idea.

Isobel agreed. Ben would charge her a fee based on hours to negotiate the property deal, and a $3000 fee to do her a financial plan plus Jasper's needs. This seemed fair, and they agreed the bill would be settled upon receipt of the land sale proceeds.

They shook hands and walked toward the door. Jasper was grateful beyond words for Ben's part in his new-found future. He shook his hand heartily and looked him directly in the eye. 'Mate, if you ever need anything, let me know.'

Ben smiled. 'I might take you up on that, actually. One of my kids needs coaching for rugby. Are you up to giving him a few pointers?'

'More than happy. Would love to,' replied Jasper, and they agreed to a time the following weekend when Jasper would meet him at the local footy grounds. With that, they parted ways and Jasper took his mother to the local coffee shop to celebrate. They toasted each other with their cappuccini, and Jasper's mum enjoyed a custard tart while Jasper gulped down a bacon and egg roll. They both felt hopeful about the future. It felt good to have a plan, and be confident they could achieve it. Seeing Ben had given them both peace of mind, and had them looking forward to what was next.

# Chapter 22

# 'The Breakfast Club' meets again

It had been more than 4 weeks since the reunion, and the lives of all six friends had been hectic. Since their meetings with Ben, each had gone on with their day-to-day lives, as well as completing tasks associated with getting what they wanted from life longer term, meaning they were even busier.

Brad couldn't believe it when Josie reminded him the reunion was exactly a month ago. He had been working solidly from his Sydney office, as well as spending time daily with his parents and most nights with Josie.

They had talked on the phone with Karen and Russ, but mainly it was Karen talking to Josie about her new business idea.

'We need to blow off some steam, babe,' said Josie, before suggesting they organise all six of them getting together. Brad went one further and suggested a whole weekend away in three weeks' time. He had to fly to a quick meeting in London and visit his San Fran office before then, but he was used to air travel and his private plane made things pretty civilised. He rang his EA, Rachel, and asked her to come up with something special for the six of them.

She didn't disappoint. She booked two nights at Wolgan Valley in the Blue Mountains — a luxury mountain villa with three bedrooms, pool and butler. She even chartered a helicopter to get them there.

Josie rang Karen and Jayne to break the good news. She relied on Russ to tell Jasper, but she knew he wouldn't say no.

'Are you serious?' squealed Jayne. She had always wanted to go there, and the thought of a free weekend with a chopper ride and high school friends — plus no kids — had her delirious.

Karen let out an expletive and whooped over the phone while yelling to Russ to pack his bags. What a fantastic opportunity to be like teenagers again.

The kids were organised to be with grandparents, and the Friday was taken off work. Everybody was in.

The weeks raced by and it was soon time to meet for the flight to the villa. Josie and Brad made sure they were there first, so they could organise drinks and ensure their friends enjoyed the full experience of the private airfield. They knew what a big deal this would be, and were excited to be able to organise such an amazing trip.

Jasper and Jayne came in an Uber together, as did Karen and Russ. Within minutes of clinking their champagne flutes, the six of them were in the helicopter and heading toward the mountains. The view was spectacular and they all hung over the windows taking in this magnificent part of the world. In only 25 minutes they landed, and Karen gasped as she caught her first view of the incredible resort.

'Paradise,' she whispered and Russ grabbed her hand. This was going to be an incredible weekend.

A staff member greeted them and they all piled their bags into a golf cart, to be transported to their private villa. They decided to walk the short distance from the airfield and take in the views. Their guide talked to them about the dining experience that evening, the horse riding they could do tomorrow if they wished, and the private pool and spa that were ready and waiting.

They got to the villa and each couple quickly found their room. Jayne threw her bag on the king size bed, and looked shyly at Jasper. 'Guess we are bunking together,' she blushed, and Jasper whistled softly.

'Let's just see how things go — no pressure,' he said. He would be more than happy to just hold her and be in the same room as her. They had talked many times on the phone and via text, but this would be the first time they had spent a full night together since the reunion.

Sexual tension filled the air, and Jasper quickly walked out of the room before it became obvious what he was thinking. Jayne took a moment to fluff her hair in the mirror and adjust her push-up bra. It had been a long time since she'd felt desired, and in her skinny jeans and knee-high boots, she thought she looked pretty damn good. She was going to enjoy the time with Jasper and she knew where it would lead. She was looking forward to it.

Russ and Karen threw themselves on their massive bed and giggled. 'How lucky are we!' Russ exclaimed, as he rolled over to give his wife a kiss. He grabbed her breast and gave it a squeeze. He knew there was a pretty good chance he was getting lucky tonight.

Instead of pushing his hand away like she usually did, Karen rolled into him, and kissed him long and hard on the mouth. She felt younger, lighter.

Before it went too far, they decided it would be rude if they didn't go back out to the main living area and join the others. They got there to find Jasper and Jayne mixing a drink at the bar, and Brad and Josie in their robes, ready to hit the hot tub.

Karen shuddered for a moment at the thought of Brad Malone getting an eyeful of her chunky white thighs, but then shrugged. Too late to be doing anything about it now, and she had no intention of dieting this weekend when they had five-star chefs catering for them!

She and Russ went back to get their swimmers on, while Jasper and Jayne settled into the deep leather couches in front of the open fire and the magnificent 180-degree view of the mountains. They had made each other a martini, and now were happily sitting together admiring the beauty of it all.

Brad and Josie got into the pool-length hot tub and let the temperature of the water seep into their muscles. Josie felt herself relax in a way she had not for a long time, as the steam dampened her hair and Brad's arms encircled her.

She had enjoyed their nights together more than she cared to admit, and had fallen back in love with Brad deeply. While he had extended his time working in Australia for another month, he had travelled quite a bit, and she wondered when he would need to go back to his base in the United States. Her life would not be the same without him, and she felt a little scared of how she would cope with him gone. She had never been dependent on a man in her life and her work life was as busy as ever, but spending her nights with Brad left her content in a way she had not been before. Whether they went out together or stayed in, she enjoyed her time with him completely.

She watched with amusement while Karen tried to enter the hot tub still wearing her robe. She knew her best friend would be paranoid about her thighs. She had heard her whinging enough times about them over the years. At the last minute, Karen flung off the robe, hitting Russ in the head. Josie laughed out loud as she watched Russ stumble into the spa, extracting his face from Karen's robe.

She gracefully moved toward Karen and lay back next to her best friend, staring at the glass ceiling and the gorgeous sky above them. Russ waded toward Brad with two beers in hand and handed one over. They clinked bottles and took a long swallow each — nothing better than beer in a spa.

The conversation ranged from what they wanted to do that weekend to what they were working on, and what they had been doing since their last meeting. They all talked about Ben, and what a massive impact he'd had. Russ filled Josie and Brad in on their meeting, and Karen talked about her new business. Josie and Brad were thrilled that things were going so well for their friends.

Brad gave them an update on his mother, and how much time they had been spending together. While it didn't make up for the years of angst, he was incredibly grateful Ben had given him the heads up about his mother's cancer. He would have never forgiven himself for not reconciling before her health declined.

Josie smiled at Brad, and commented on how happy she was that Brad was getting on so well with his mum. There was still some friction, but with his mother's strong personality, not to mention his own, it was a miracle that they had reconciled their differences so soon. They'd spent time talking about the past and things that had happened, and moments from Brad's childhood his mother was incredibly proud of.

All these discussions were changing the way Brad saw his childhood, and healing some very old hurt around what value his parents put on him as a person, rather than as a reflection of their own achievement. He finally understood just how deeply these ideas had affected him, despite all his success as an adult.

Ben seemed to be the centre point of everyone's new outlook, and the four of them decided to do something special to thank him. 'How about we send him here?' asked Brad, to which Russ and Karen remained silent. They couldn't really afford to be contributing to a holiday for Ben that was at least $2000 a night.

'Why don't you cook a dinner for him, Karen?' asked Josie, sensing her friend would feel uncomfortable not contributing, but couldn't afford this place.

'Definitely! I'll ask his wife, and we can all meet at our house,' enthused Karen, at once confident she could contribute. She could never keep up financially with Josie, let alone Brad, but she could cook a great meal, and she knew Ben would enjoy it.

Just then Jasper cannonballed into the spa, soaking them all and leaving Josie's hair flat on her face. She looked up with murder in her eyes. He was still as annoying as ever.

Jasper noticed her filthy look and quickly moved over to Brad and Russ. Jayne climbed in with an apologetic look and three glasses of champagne, which calmed Josie down considerably.

Jayne told Josie how grateful she was to be here. She could never afford a place like this — it just didn't make sense to spend what was her monthly rent money on a couple of nights here. But to be here and enjoy it with friends was unbelievable.

She filled Josie and Karen in on her job research. Working in a legal office as a public defender was probably out of the question — the pay wasn't great and the hours were long — but she was thinking of starting her own consultancy, and she thought her current employer would become her first client. She could earn more consulting, and work her hours around commitments with the kids, even with her parents helping.

'I have to say though, I'm terrified,' she admitted. 'It's a lot of change, in a short space of time. I don't know if I'll cut it as a consultant, or even if I can get more clients than one.' Josie could see the fear in her eyes, and understood entirely how terrifying failure could be. And the older you got, the harder it was to bounce back from it. 'Jayne, if you are as good as I suspect you are, I'll introduce you around. I know a lot of companies in the business community that could do with some outsourced advice on things, at a cost-effective rate.'

Jayne's heart leaped into her chest — having someone the status of Josie offering to introduce her around was certainly going to help her win work. As long as Jayne could offer a great standard, she knew she would do Josie proud. She gave Josie a spontaneous hug, her champagne glass dangling precariously near their heads, and then pulled away solemnly. 'If you believe in me enough to refer me, I promise on my life I won't let you down. I will work 120 per cent to make sure you never regret it.'

'I know that,' said Josie in a warm tone. 'If you are anything like most mums I know, you'll work twice as hard as anyone else in the room.'

Jayne nodded happily, feeling much more confident at the change she was going to undertake in her life. While it was a risk, the opportunity was too good to pass up. The ability to give the girls some sort of legacy, like her parents were giving her, was extremely important to her. For the first time in her career, she felt like she might be able to provide that legacy without a husband to help.

Karen admitted she also knew how Jayne was feeling. While she felt a lot of excitement around starting her own online business, she had no idea if it was going to work. And if it failed, she would be really embarrassed because a lot of people knew about it—it would be a very public failure. The other mums would no doubt gossip and bitch as if they'd known all along someone like Karen couldn't run a business.

'The fear of failing at this is almost bigger than the excitement of doing it,' Karen admitted to the others, a look of sheer terror coming over her face. 'Plus I'm supposed to be contributing to our family financially. I'm worried I'll end up costing us more than I make.'

Jayne reminded her that Karen was lucky because Russ supported her, and so did her kids.

'I wouldn't measure your success on anything at first but how much you enjoy it,' Josie advised. 'Doing something you're passionate about will add value to people, and you'll make money. You need to give it time, and let go of any early expectations it will be a big money spinner. You need to learn first.'

As usual, Karen was grateful for her friendship with Josie. When it came to business, there wasn't a lot that Josie didn't know and she was always generous with her advice. She noticed, however, Josie still looked tired. She knew her well enough to know her make-up covered the bags under her eyes.

'You look tired, babe—is Brad keeping you up at night?' she teased. Josie smiled guiltily. 'He certainly is,' she joked, but also went on to admit that work was still incredibly demanding. She'd been thinking a lot about what Ben had said about selling equity to her key staff, and she'd decided she was going to do it. 'I don't love the hustle the way I used to,' she admitted. 'I'm tired because I want to slow down. I still want to work, but solving one or two challenges would be a helluvalot easier than solving ten at once.'

Karen and Jayne could both see how much Josie needed to change her working life—before something happened to her health. The kind of stress she was under could really affect your physical and mental health as you got older. Josie also filled them in that she was thinking of selling some of her investment properties, so she didn't need to make quite as much money to have her world tick over.

Neither Jayne nor Karen could even comprehend what it was like to have to earn hundreds of thousands of dollars every month to pay for your business and life. It was incredible that Josie had built it—but it was also very understandable that the pressure of it was enough to weigh Josie down. Josie shrugged her shoulders and turned her attention to the men. She was admiring Brad's firm shoulders and arms—he really was a gorgeous specimen. Karen and Jayne, however, were looking at their men for entirely different reasons, and shaking their heads. Jasper was trying to pull down Russ's shorts and they were horse playing around like teenagers.

'Helllloooo,' Karen called out in her stern voice, and the two turned around guiltily. When they got together it was inevitable they become teenagers again.

After a few more raised eyebrows from the ladies, the two of them quickly realised it was time to get out of the spa and act like grown-ups again. They guiltily filed out, followed by Brad.

It was very hard for Jayne and Karen not to ogle him — a body like his was rarely seen on the school run or in the office.

Josie noticed and smirked to herself. She was still perving too!

Brad must have known all three women were staring, but to his credit he pretended to be unaware and wrapped a robe around himself straight after getting out of the water, much to the disappointment of the female audience.

Jasper turned around and noticed Jayne's look, and quickly moved to usher her over to the fireplace, glass of wine in hand, before she had any more time to check Brad out. Jasper was fit and he had always been athletic, but Brad Malone took that to a whole new level. The guy was Hollywood fit, and the less Jayne saw of that the better as far as Jasper was concerned. Not to mention the guy was seriously loaded. Jasper knew he couldn't compete on any level with Brad. He was conflicted about that — he actually liked Brad and thought he was a decent guy. He didn't want to feel threatened by him, but it was hard not to — especially when Jasper was considering changing his whole life and becoming a student again.

He was feeling more trepidation the closer it got to enrolment time. He had three months to lock it all in — and then he was living with his mum and going to school with no real income. The trifecta. He kept thinking about his mother's discussion with the developer. Nothing had been locked in yet, but Jasper kept thinking that maybe that $800k could be better used to buy him a unit and a new car. Maybe even a holiday for Jayne and him. The thought of putting his part of it away for retirement was not the most appealing, even though what Ben had said made perfect sense at the time. He wanted a better life now — not in 25 years. He felt like he had waited long enough. He shook his head quickly and focused back on the now. Jayne looked gorgeous with her hair all wispy from the spa and a healthy glow from the fire. He needed to remember to enjoy the here and now, rather than comparing himself to others and stressing about his future.

Russ was sipping red wine contentedly and lounging on the thick rug in front of the fire with Karen, who was dreamily staring at a magnificent mountain view. He had enjoyed horsing around with Jasper. It felt good to have fun again, and feel younger and more carefree. The thought of staying in the same job didn't exactly fill him with joy, but he also knew he owed it to Karen to give her a chance to do something for her. Sure, it was intended to make the family money, but what he knew it could really do was give her a sense of purpose and provide a challenge that she hadn't been able to have in years. She had made their children her full-time priority—which was why they were all thriving.

It was time, however, for her to have more. She had lost some of the light in her eyes in the past few years, and he knew that cooking, cleaning and running kids around wasn't exactly keeping her stimulated. Her life was incredibly exhausting and never-ending, and it was also thankless a lot of the time. Her role was definitely in the background, making it all work, rather than up-front. Karen deserved her time up-front, and he hadn't seen her this excited in a very long time. She was waking up in the night writing down lists, and scratching out notes as she stirred dinner at the stove. Her creative juices were flowing and he knew that her being fulfilled that way would be great for her and the whole family.

Outside of having a happier wife, however, it also meant his life wasn't going to change much, at least for now. He was going to show up at the same old office and face the same people, making the same self-serving decisions day after day. He sighed into his wine glass and his eyes became slightly bleak.

Karen instantly noticed his body language change, and wondered what he was thinking about. She hoped she hadn't let him down over the past few weeks. There had been some burnt meals and unfolded washing as she focused more on her website. Russ wasn't used to that.

Russ noticed Karen watching him a little anxiously and smiled. He clinked his wine glass on hers and came back to the present. He needed to remember not to think too far ahead — it usually made him dread his future. He needed to be in the present and enjoy what was happening. It was, after all, pretty damn amazing.

Brad and Josie sat in the double armchair, snuggled into one another and sipping a fine whisky. This was pretty much bliss, and while all of them had other things weighing on their mind, they also knew that this time together was valuable and precious — rare but as necessary as breathing to feeling like a whole person again. Without the time to share, reflect and relax, life was too much of a treadmill that you could never slow down from.

'My God! Who would have thought I would miss you guys so much,' marvelled Brad, and each of them instantly felt a warm glow. He was sincere and just like them, despite who he was in the real world — he needed genuine friendship and time out to really check in. 'I'd forgotten what it was like to have real friends, with no agenda and expectations,' Brad confessed.

'I wouldn't say noooo expectations,' Jasper drawled. 'You've set the bar pretty high bringing us here. I'd say we all expect it to be an annual thing.' Josie scowled at Jasper, and Brad laughed. 'Mate, you are on. "The Breakfast Club for 40-somethings" annual get away.' They all clapped and hooted — that was a brilliant idea, and coming together year after year was going to be one of the best traditions ever. True friendship was one of the greatest joys in life — and realising that the six of them would invest in it for the next 30 years felt great.

They decided to crack the butterscotch schnapps before dinner, and Karen knew she was in for quite the hangover in the morning. But it was so worth it.

# Chapter 23

# Twenty years later

The trip to the Blue Mountains was the first of many weekends away for the six of them. And boy did they do it well, thanks to Brad. 'The Breakfast Club for 40-somethings' never went to the same place twice. From the Hunter Valley, to the Daintree and Uluru, Brad's EA organised the most incredible getaways, and each time was always just as good as the last. They laughed and confessed, and shared joys, sorrows and everything in between.

Josie ended up selling most of her business to her staff. She worked three months of the year in Sydney, and spent the rest of the time overseas with Brad. They'd married, and Josie ran Brad's philanthropic trust—which was focused on sponsoring the next generation of entrepreneurial thinkers who would then go on to run socially responsible businesses. The work was incredibly rewarding, and the trust extremely well-funded. Josie no longer felt she had to keep a treadmill going for work, and she'd made enough of her own money to never have to rely on Brad. She was grateful for this, not because Brad would begrudge her having anything—he was incredibly generous—but because she'd wanted to prove to herself that she could do it, and she had. While she no longer had the burning drive she had in her younger years, in her sixties she knew where she was best placed to have an impact, and the work she did changed thousands of lives.

She'd been able to show her parents her amazing work with the trust before they died more than 10 years ago. She was grateful they could see it, because making money had never really impressed them. Making a difference definitely did, and they were incredibly proud of her.

Brad's empire continued to grow under his brilliant stewardship. He became known for being a philanthropist as much as a businessman, and got great joy out of working with Josie on their educational trust to help give children the opportunity for education — from primary school to university. They then funded these students to start their own socially responsible businesses. It was an inter-generational philanthropic trust and would last well after he and Josie were gone.

He named the program after his mother, who had passed away a year after that first reunion. Brad still felt a touch of sadness when he thought of her, but he was incredibly grateful for the time they'd had after Ben had told him of her illness. His dad died two years later, and Brad knew then he was on his own. Of course, he still had a brother, whom he made a lot more effort to spend time with. He and Josie never had their own kids, so the kids who benefited from their philanthropy became more important in their lives the older they got.

Karen and Russ had moved to the central coast a couple of years ago. Karen's parents had left her the house, and they'd decided to sell up their Sydney home once the kids were all grown up and turn most of the $3 million they received into an allocated pension. This meant they got to go on holidays overseas every year, and spoil their grandkids when they visited. Karen's online business had done well — she had launched cook books and school planners off the site after a couple of years, and ended up making more than $100 000 per year in sales. Russ was able to change jobs four years after Karen started, and ended up working at the University of Newcastle as a lecturer in accounting. While it didn't pay what finance did, it was incredibly rewarding. He loved it and was glad he had given Karen the space and time to grow her business in the first place. He barely remembered the sacrifice now.

They had kept Ben on as their financial adviser, and now had trusts set up for each of their kids, with enough money to give them a start—and a plan on how their estate was to be divided. Each of their kids would have some security as they got older, and that made Russ and Karen incredibly proud. As parents they had done their best to give their kids every opportunity they could. Now that their children were adults, they knew they wouldn't have to struggle so much with money, and that they would have a legacy from their parents.

Jayne and Jasper dated for a few years and then broke up as the best of friends. Nothing really happened, they just fizzled out. They still got on like a house on fire when 'The Breakfast Club' met again, but booked separate rooms and became platonic friends.

Jayne met someone soon after in the new law firm where she'd started working as consultant. They dated for a few years before he proposed, and they were happily married, living in an apartment near the city. They both still worked and intended on practising law for at least another 5 years. Jayne's parents had sold their house a couple of years after they first met with Ben. They had used the majority of the sale to get themselves into a retirement village and were still going strong in their nineties. Jayne was glad she had been given $200 000 when they sold their house to put into her super fund and, 18 years on, she now had a tidy nest egg and almost $800 000 in super. It was a lot more than she'd expected, and with her husband's income combined with hers, her life was financially secure. She would never travel the world in first class, but she had a comfortable life.

Her twins went on to start an online make-up business together and were doing well. She was incredibly proud. Her ex had died of a liver disease a couple of years ago. The girls went to his funeral, but they knew little of the man they called Dad, and he left no financial legacy at all.

Jasper had inherited his mother's home eight years ago. She had given him the proceeds of selling her back block, and he had bought himself a one-bedroom unit in a suburb close by. While Ben had cautioned him on buying it, he wanted to be near his mum. He had dropped out of university after the first year. He just couldn't do the study and he quickly fell behind in his workload. Knowing he didn't have what it took to be a teacher, he got a job as the soccer co-ordinator for primary schools in the region. He was still around sport, and helped the kids with confidence and skills. He did a lot with the community and was a much-loved figure in local soccer. The job paid $70 000 but he made it work. He'd married a single soccer mum, and was divorced five years later, meaning he'd had to sell the unit and pay half to his ex because he hadn't organised the pre-nup like Ben had advised.

He'd gone back to renting until his mother died. He'd then sold her house and was living on the proceeds. He bought a smaller townhouse near his work, and Ben had helped him invest the rest in super. He knew he had to keep working as long as he could, because what he had in super wouldn't last if he was to live until he was 90.

As for Ben, he was chuffed to stay in contact with them all. He still had his practice, which had grown to a network of advice firms. He was the chairman now and loved watching the difference his people made every day in the lives of their clients. He had no regrets about his life—he had done exactly as he wanted, and would continue to contribute for as many years as he could. He had grandkids and many friends, and his life was full.

So 'The Breakfast Club for 40-somethings' continued to meet every year. Looking back to when they first met back up at the reunion, they realised that life was nothing like they'd imagined it. They'd had ups and downs, and different challenges, and each of them had gone down very different paths. But their friendship remained the same. The choices they'd made in their forties had defined the next 20 years. They had reinvented their futures and were now living the lives those choices had created.

They had taken to writing a message to the next inhabitants of where they were staying, as a signature sign-off every year.

This year's wisdom was particularly poignant and even Jasper had to agree with it.

If you're finding yourself in your forties, and wondering if this is it, know there's more. Make deliberate choices and seek the very best in advice. You can reinvent your life. We know, because we did.

Sincerely yours,
The Breakfast Club

# Author's diagnosis

I hope you enjoyed sharing the lives of 'The Breakfast Club for 40-somethings' as much as I did in creating them. For me, writing this book has been both a joy and a challenge—but an important part of my life purpose is telling stories that bring the finance industry closer to you, and helping you reach your financial and life goals.

As for the characters, did you relate to what their unlearn pillars were? While many had multiple pillars to unlearn, each had at least one major unlearning. Some they carried from their childhood, others were unacknowledged or disguised as things they wanted, so they didn't even know they were holding them back.

For Josie, desire was her Achilles heel, and she had the sense to change her spending habits before it took a greater toll on her. She also had the wisdom to know when it was time to change. For so many of us, change is frightening—and it seems the older we get, the more frightening change becomes. While Josie experienced fear, she moved forward and reinvented her future.

For Jasper, focus was his big unlearn pillar. Living from party to party, and dead-end job to dead-end job had not given him a present he was proud of. He did get more focused in the end, while still making mistakes about money along the way. The belief pillar was also a factor, with the lessons he learned from his father never really leaving him — and these always led him to choose the easy road, even when it wasn't the best. While he did seek advice, he didn't always take it, and lived with the consequences of his choices.

For Russ and Karen, time played a big part in their unlearning. They knew they needed to do something about diversifying their income and funding their retirement. It could have gone either way for them, but Karen fought to unlearn her childhood beliefs that she was never going to earn money, and put herself out there to start a business. This made all the difference for both of them when it succeeded.

Russ was also strategic about time, deciding not to chase another job and more money, and instead give Karen the opportunity to succeed. As a reward, he got to spend more time with his children and share the load of funding the family. He even ended up in his dream job. Their decision to move to the coast meant that life was less expensive, and their retirement dollars stretched further. The fact they were able to leave their children a financial legacy was the icing on the cake. They are a great example of good long-term planning advice in action.

Brad also unlearned a major lesson in time from his mother's illness. No matter the financial success he had achieved, success in life was about more than just money. Forming authentic relationships and family understanding was a big step forward for the billionaire in the group. While people assume that billionaires have a fantasy life, they can often forget what it takes to get there and the crushing workload to maintain it. Brad could have missed the chance to reconcile with his mother — something he would have carried with him for life. By recognising he had to unlearn time, and move quickly to spend time with his parents, he avoided carrying a lifetime of regret.

Jayne also unlearned focus — with hers being too narrow and too focused on kids and marriage. She learned that putting her focus on other people to make her happy was an unrewarding strategy. Instead, Jayne broadened her focus by finding a way to earn more, and to keep working long after her children had grown up. She also worked on her belief pillar, by believing more in what she was capable of and what she was worth. She took smart advice on putting the money her parents gave her away for her retirement, and it gave her choices in the next phase of her life. It also allowed her to think about doing the same for her kids.

Acknowledging just how much she would need in her super was an important step for Jayne (and, indeed, her father). As Ben pointed out, with people living longer after retirement, the current government support (such as it is) just won't be around in 20 years' time. Retirement will need to be self-funded and thinking you can simply sell the family home and downsize won't be enough of a strategy (as Karen and Russ worked out).

Of course, the big decider for all our characters was their action plan—which they could not have achieved without the help of their friend Ben, the financial planner. We all need a Ben in our lives. Someone we can trust, confide in and take comfort from as we navigate the tricky waters of getting older. I can honestly say that having a good financial planner working on my family action plan has made an enormous difference to our lives. Don't think Ben is a one-off or simple work of fiction. Many financial planners out there are just like him—completely trustworthy and with your best interests at heart. My hope is that by reading this book and understanding more about the role a good financial planner can play, you will gain similar outcomes to myself and the characters in this book.

What pillars do you need to unlearn? How are you going to put your ideas into action? After 24 years of working in the finance industry, I have learned a lot about money. But to ask you to *unlearn* money as a first step is a new approach. If you want to go deeper, visit my website (vanessastoykov.com) and take my quiz on what you need to unlearn about money. It will provide insight into yourself and your behaviours, and set you on a path to look at the next 20 years of your life differently.

You will also find a guide to finding the right financial planner (just like Jayne's dad found) and a journal to help you record your longer term goals on what you want your life to be like. Reinventing your life takes time and planning, but remember — it's worth it.

If you want to know more about growing your wealth outside of property, my site will also lead you to video learning on investing, and my channel 9 TV show *Learn from the Money Masters*, where I take celebrities through a real-life money masterclass.

It is never too late to unlearn your money habits and take the time to invest in yourself and build an action plan to move toward your goals. Whether you are in your thirties, forties, fifties or beyond, if you are reading this book, you are capable of changing your reality. The earlier you start, the better the outcome.

Go on. Reinvent your life. Live as you imagine. The possibilities are endless.

Until the next story,
Vanessa

# About the author

With over two decades of experience in the wealth creation space, Vanessa Stoykov is a highly respected finance industry thought leader with a passion for storytelling.

She is the Founder of *No More Practice Education,* a leading on-line financial education hub which trains more than 20,000 finance professionals, Founder and Chief Executive of production house *evolution media group* and creator of the Channel Nine's *Learn from the Money Masters: The Investment Series.*

Vanessa believes that to truly grow long term wealth, people need to UNLEARN everything they think they know about money. As such, she is dedicated to helping professionals and financial advisors learn how to grow wealth by focusing on 'educating the educators' with new techniques to assist them in better communicating and serving the wider community.

Vanessa writes for more than 40,000 people each week in her own subscribed blogs, is a regular contributor of *Morningstar,* one of the largest investment research houses in the world, a regular columnist for NewsCorp's Body+Soul and can be seen on everything from *Channel 10's Studio 10, to News.com.au, Daily Mail, CEO Magazine, Dynamic Business and Money Magazine*

But now, at the age of 44 Vanessa is even more committed than ever to telling stories that actually matter, and to helping anyone and everyone better their lives.

Outside of the corporate space, Vanessa enjoys spending time in the Blue Mountains with her husband Woody and their three sons, and visiting her hometown of Gunnedah, where she first realised her passion for storytelling by hiding a torch in her bedroom and reading under the doona well after bedtime.